D1126832

The Empire Builders

THE ART OF SEWING
THE OLD WEST
THE EMERGENCE OF MAN
THE AMERICAN WILDERNESS
THE TIME-LIFE ENCYCLOPEDIA OF GARDENING
LIFE LIBRARY OF PHOTOGRAPHY
THIS FABULOUS CENTURY
FOODS OF THE WORLD
TIME-LIFE LIBRARY OF AMERICA
TIME-LIFE LIBRARY OF ART
GREAT AGES OF MAN
LIFE SCIENCE LIBRARY
THE LIFE HISTORY OF THE UNITED STATES
TIME READING PROGRAM
LIFE NATURE LIBRARY
LIFE WORLD LIBRARY
FAMILY LIBRARY:
THE TIME-LIFE BOOK OF THE FAMILY CAR
THE TIME-LIFE FAMILY LEGAL GUIDE
THE TIME-LIFE BOOK OF FAMILY FINANCE

The Emergence of Man

The Empire Builders

by Jim Hicks
and the Editors
of TIME-LIFE BOOKS

TIME-LIFE BOOKS
New York

Valuable assistance was given by the following departments and individuals of Time Inc.: Editorial Production, Norman Airey; Library, Benjamin Lightman; Picture Collection, Doris O'Neil; Photographic Laboratory, George Karas; TIME-LIFE News Service, Murray J. Gart; Correspondents Margot Hapgood and Dorothy Bacon (London), Elisabeth Kraemer (Bonn), Mehmet Ali Kislali (Ankara), Ann Natanson (Rome), Maria Vincenza Aloisi (Paris), Helga Kohl (Athens), Giovanna Breu and Brooke Gillespie (Chicago).

The Author: JIM HICKS, a former staff member of LIFE magazine, is a freelance writer living in London. While working for LIFE, he traveled extensively in the Near East and North Africa, where he became interested in ancient civilizations. He has written numerous articles and has twice received reporting awards from The National Headliners Club.

The Consultants: OLIVER ROBERT GURNEY, Fellow of Magdalen College and Professor at Oxford University, has specialized in Assyriology since 1934. He studied the Hittite language at Berlin University; since then he has written many articles and books on the Hittites. They include the comprehensive work *The Hittites,* first published in 1952, and *The Geography of the Hittite Empire* (written in collaboration with John Garstang) in 1959. He has also participated in excavations of ancient sites in Turkey.
HARRY A. HOFFNER, JR., Associate Professor of Hittitology at The Oriental Institute of the University of Chicago, is the author of several works on the language and literature of the Hittites, including *An English-Hittite Glossary* and *Alimenta Hethaeorum* (Foodstuffs of the Hittites). The editors of *The Empire Builders* are indebted to Professor Hoffner for supplying them with English translations of many of the Hittite texts quoted in this book.

The Cover: Overshadowed by the larger-than-life sculpture of a warrior god, a Hittite soldier directs weary Syrian prisoners through an arched gate into the empire's fortified capital, Hattusa. The painting is by Michael Hampshire, who also provided the illustrations for pages 25-31 and 105-113.

Published simultaneously in Canada.
Library of Congress catalogue card number 74-75832.

Contents

Introduction

Ask the next person you meet who the Egyptians or the Babylonians were and the odds are that the answer will reveal at least a nodding familiarity with the historic roles of those ancient peoples in the development of man. But ask the same person who the Hittites were and you are almost certain to draw a blank. Yet the Hittites were an equally mighty power, who once held sway over an empire—centered in the wind-swept highlands of what is now Turkey—that stretched over much of the Near East before it vanished abruptly, for mysterious reasons, more than 3,000 years ago.

The Hittites have been rediscovered only within the last 100 years or so. In tracing and unearthing the impressive remains of their capital, the fortified city of Hattusa, with its enormous palaces and temples, archeologists at first substantiated the existence of a powerful, urbane and ambitious people. But broken artifacts and tumbled walls could tell only part of their story. Without written records, the ruins of any dead civilization are mute: only through their own writings can a long-vanished people come truly alive again, are they able to give voice to their motivating ideas and principles.

Fortunately, the Hittites left behind in Hattusa and elsewhere a wealth of documents inscribed in hieroglyphs or cuneiform. After decades of patient effort by decipherers, these can now be read. As a Hittitologist, I have translated many of them myself. They reveal the Hittites beyond their material and historical achievements: the rivals of the Egyptians, the destroyers of Babylon. They make them appear in flesh-and-blood terms as a people with very human problems and concerns, whose views on a wide variety of matters sometimes seem surprisingly in advance of their time.

Their laws tell us how they sought to settle grievances not by retaliation but by reasonable payments to compensate for damages. Their treaties show how fair-minded they could be in dealing with vanquished enemies. From their myths we see how they explained the seemingly capricious and unpredictable side of the natural world as the work of a large—1,000-member—community of gods and goddesses with lively personalities and a sense of humor. From their prayers we come to admire their piety, uncompromising frankness and moral sensitivity. And from the records of their numerous rituals we learn something about their personal lives and how they handled a broad spectrum of complaints ranging from mental distress to physical illness.

Thus, the author of this book has been able to draw upon the Hittites' own writings to assemble a remarkable and fascinating portrait of a people who built a great empire that for too long was ignored—indeed, forgotten—by history.

Harry A. Hoffner, Jr.
The Oriental Institute of the
University of Chicago

Chapter One: The Lost Empire

In the long and fascinating story of man's emergence there are many surprises, but few quite so astonishing as the rediscovery, in recent times, of an entire empire—that of the ancient Hittites. Once as important and as powerful as the Egyptians, the Hittites all but disappeared from memory, and only now are being restored to their rightful place in history. Among other things, they were one of the first peoples to build an empire; moreover they bound their diverse realm together with laws and treaties surprisingly modern in character.

People called Hittites have long been known, of course, through the Bible. Characters bearing that name slipped on and off the stage in several familiar Old Testament dramas—a tribe of bit players who carried spears in crowd scenes and on occasion were given small speaking parts, along with such other extras as the Jebusites and the Amorites. For example, it was "Ephron the Hittite" who sold Abraham a cave in which to bury his wife Sarah. Uriah, whose wife, Bathsheba, was seen bathing by the hot-blooded King David, was also called a Hittite. And, as is well known, Uriah died in the second act.

Since the Old Testament was written centuries after the Hittite Empire ended in 1200 B.C., the Biblical "Hittites" could only have been lesser lights who had preserved the name and remnants of Hittite culture. Thus they served to establish firmly the fuzzy notion, still held by many persons, of the Hittites as a group of Palestinian tribesmen of little importance.

Until nearly a century ago even historians could add very little to change the picture. But as archeologists began unearthing impressive Hittite remains in Turkey and northern Syria, and as scholars gradually learned to decipher Hittite writings inscribed on clay tablets and engraved on stone monuments, they were amazed to learn the truth about this extraordinary people.

The Hittites, far from being a minor group of tribesmen, at one time ranked among the supreme lords of civilization: they were not only a colossus of a nation compared to the Old Testament Israelites but a giant strong enough to sack storied Babylon and to challenge successfully the authority of mighty Egypt.

Historians now know that nearly 1,700 years before the birth of Christ, the Hittites were founding their capital, Hattusa, in Anatolia, Turkey's central plateau region. Hattusa, which overlay the ruins of an older city, flourished for nearly 500 years as the administrative and religious hub of Hittite life and at its zenith covered some 400 acres, making it much larger than the contemporary Assyrian capital of Assur in northern Mesopotamia. Dominated by palaces and temples, it was unlike any other known city of the ancient world. Standing 3,000 feet above sea level on a rugged tableland, snow-covered in winter, scorched by the blazing sun in summer and ringed by mountains infested with wolves and bears, the Hittites' capital bore an anachronistic similarity to medieval fortresses. And a fortress it was. The site it occupied was itself a natural stronghold, a steeply sloping tongue of land set off from the surrounding country on one side by a deep protective gorge (the modern Turkish town that sits below its ruins is

The running figures of four minor Hittite gods—a detail of a relief on the wall of a sanctuary near the Hittite capital of Hattusa—record the Hittites' own dress and physical traits. Stocky, with noses that slant unindented from the brow, they wear short tunics. The conical hats are the emblem of godhood; the single horns on them indicate low rank.

called Bogazköy, "gorge village") and on the other by a narrow valley. Also guarding the city were its double, crenelated walls—built of massive stone, topped by brick battlements, pierced by archlike gateways and punctuated at intervals by tall towers.

Even the tumbled, half-buried ruins of Hattusa are a stirring sight. "A visit to the actual remains of the Hittite capital," wrote British historian Seton Lloyd, "with its ruined palaces and temples, monumental sculptures and the four-mile circuit of its ponderously constructed walls cannot fail to leave one with the conviction that this city has been the cradle and home of a great imperial people."

From this impressively urbanized base the Hittites fanned out over much of the known world, bringing kings to their knees and carrying Hittite hegemony from the Aegean to beyond the Euphrates in Mesopotamia, north to the Black Sea and south to the plains of Syria, where their armies encountered, contested and rolled back the borders of the rival Egyptian empire. In an approach unusual for their era, they relied nearly as heavily on their diplomats as on their warriors: whenever possible they preferred to make their conquests by means of threat and negotiation rather than by force of arms.

It is not solely the surprising reach of Hittite power that makes these long-forgotten people so fascinating. The thousands of inscribed clay tablets painstakingly recovered by archeologists from the ruins of Hattusa and patiently translated by epigraphists (who first had to decipher languages that no man had read or spoken for 3,000 years) have revealed other remarkable aspects of the Hittites' social, political, religious and intellectual life. The writings not only illuminate such weighty matters as the rights of kings and queens, and treaties with foreign powers, but they also shed light on details as mundane as the price a man could legally ask for the sale of a full-grown cow or what a housewife might expect to pay for a length of linen cloth.

For all their diligence in reconstructing the Hittite past, however, the experts have yet to come up with several large and important pieces needed to complete the picture. Where, for instance, did these empire builders come from? This unanswered question is made all the more tantalizing because of an especially astounding fact that has been discovered about them: unlike the Near Eastern peoples they conquered, they were not of Semitic origin. The study of their writings has shown that they spoke an Indo-European language, belonging to the same family as English, Latin, Greek, the Celtic and Slavic tongues, and Sanskrit. Where the Indo-European languages began their development is a matter of scholarly debate, but many philologists see the weight of evidence favoring a European birthplace.

The Hittites, then, appear to have been one of the first—if not the very first—Indo-European-speaking peoples to step into recorded history. The other possible candidates for that honor are a people known as Luwians, who spoke an Indo-European language closely related to that of the Hittites. The Luwians, however, left only a minor mark on history; they settled in the southwest of Turkey, never progressed politically beyond small states and eventually became vassals of the Hittites.

When asked not long ago where the Hittites might have first appeared, one Hittitologist waved toward the map pinned on his office wall. Vaguely indicating a vast tract of territory extending all the way from

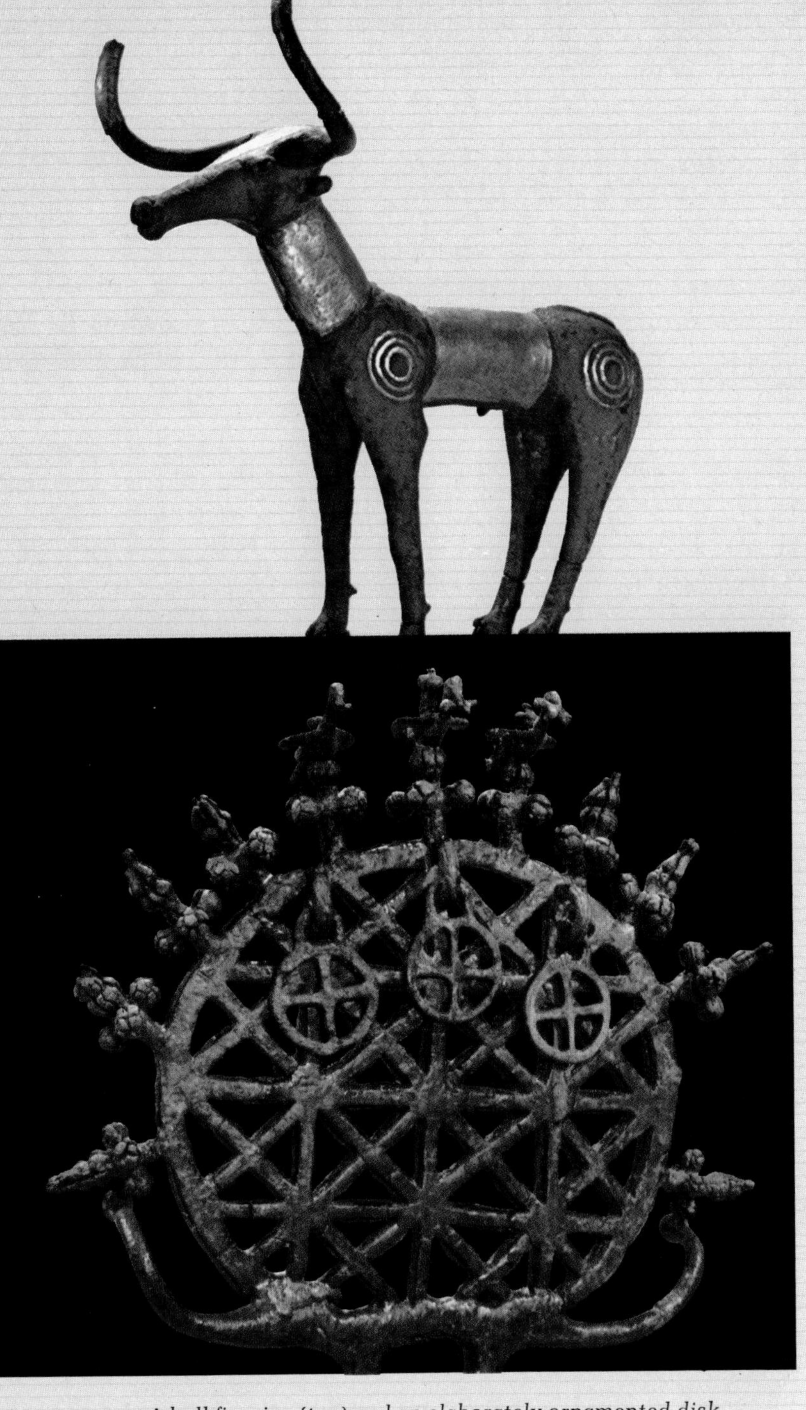

A bull figurine (top) and an elaborately ornamented disk (bottom) are among the rich finds of a culture predating by 300 years the Hittite civilization in Asia Minor. The sculptures, both of bronze and both measuring about a foot high, come from the royal tombs of Alaça Hüyük, a city that flourished from about 2300 to 2100 B.C. Puzzled archeologists, who have found nothing quite like them elsewhere, tentatively catalogue them as standards; indeed, they look as if they might have served as heads for scepters or finials for chariots. The tips of the bull's horns, the mask, the collar, the saddle and the concentric circles on the body are all fashioned of inlaid silver.

northern Europe to southern Russia and from west of the Black Sea to the Caspian and the fringe of Asia on the east, he said, in a voice reflecting the special pain that imprecision inflicts upon scholars, "Somewhere up there—presumably."

The earliest archeological inkling of the Hittites' existence comes from Asia Minor—from the Anatolian plateau, which was to become their base for imperial expansion. There, at an ancient trading center called Kanesh, known to modern Turkey as Kültepe, a group of Assyrians arrived about 1900 B.C. to establish a *karum,* or merchant colony. They imported expensive fabrics from their capital, Assur, 500 miles away, trading them to the local inhabitants for copper and other minerals with which the region was well endowed. And, like meticulous businessmen of any era, they carefully recorded contracts, loans and other details of their day-to-day transactions.

Over a period of centuries the *karum* at Kanesh was destroyed and rebuilt several times, but under the successive layers of rubble thousands of the merchants' records—inscribed in wedge-shaped cuneiform characters on clay tablets, which were often enclosed in clay envelopes—fortuitously survived, waiting to inform modern investigators of the price of fine Assyrian cloth almost 40 centuries ago and the names of the people who bought it. Some of those customers had Hittite names.

How the Hittites got to Asia Minor and what prompted them to come are problems as unresolved as their point of origin. Some historians believe that, pressed by the increase of their own population or that of neighboring peoples, they descended from southern Russia, making their way down the broad neck of land between the Black and Caspian seas and over the Caucasus ranges. Others think it more likely that they came down through the Balkans, crossing the narrow strait of the Bosporus from Europe to Asia. Whatever route they may have followed, their arrival in Asia Minor was a momentous event for what was then the civilized world.

Asia Minor, which was given that name by the Romans in the Fifth Century A.D., probably to distinguish it from the rest of the Asiatic continent, juts out between the waters of the Black and Mediterranean seas like the head of some heavy-jowled Oriental beast nosing up to Europe. Here, at this meeting place of two continents, Occident and Orient have collided repeatedly and violently in their long struggle to dominate each other. From here the Persian warrior-king Xerxes invaded Greece in 480 B.C. Later the armies of Alexander the Great trampled through in the other direction on conquests that carried them as far as India. In medieval times Turks crossed the Bosporus to march almost to the gates of Vienna. Long before these events, however, the Hittites had invaded Asia Minor in what appears to have been the first confrontation between East and West.

When the Hittites first entered the civilized world, they probably were still barbarians, and they no doubt felt that mixture of awe and contempt characteristic of the backwoodsman come to town. Archeology has shown that there were rich and sophisticated settlements in Anatolia before they arrived. Beneath the ruins of a Hittite city at Alaça Hüyük in central Turkey, and again at a site near the Sea of Marmara, tombs have yielded exquisite objects that hint at the cultural refinement of the pre-Hittite residents. Among the artifacts are lavishly decorated ceremonial weapons (including a dagger with a blade of iron, more valuable than gold to the Early Bronze Age people who buried it), a gold filigree diadem and gold drinking vessels, as well as gold toilet articles, jewelry and other ornaments.

If the rude newcomers from the north were impressed by such wealth and achievement, they also seem to have discerned that in some ways they were superior to the local inhabitants. The Hittites were a vigorous, practical people, politically shrewd and militarily adept. The communities of their Anatolian predecessors, judging from the archeological remains and later Hittite writings, were small and competitive, with no princeling ruling more than a few thousand subjects. Some of these city-states occasionally pooled their strength in alliances of limited duration, but there is no evidence of any true unification until it was imposed by the Hittites.

Exactly how they established their dominance is not clear. Perhaps their drive for power was instigated by envy and a desire to possess the wealth and to control the trade routes of the rich communities around them. The Hittite army in those early days probably numbered only a few thousand men, however, and certainly did not sweep across Asia Minor in a sudden, sustained march of conquest. The advance seems to have taken centuries and was doubtless a combination of military successes and gradual absorption of indigenous peoples and their cultures. In the process, the Hittites were not loath to pick up any local custom, belief or technique —whether from friend, neighbor or subject—that they found valuable. They adopted the cuneiform writing system of the Babylonians around 1650 B.C. and used it along with their own system of hiero-

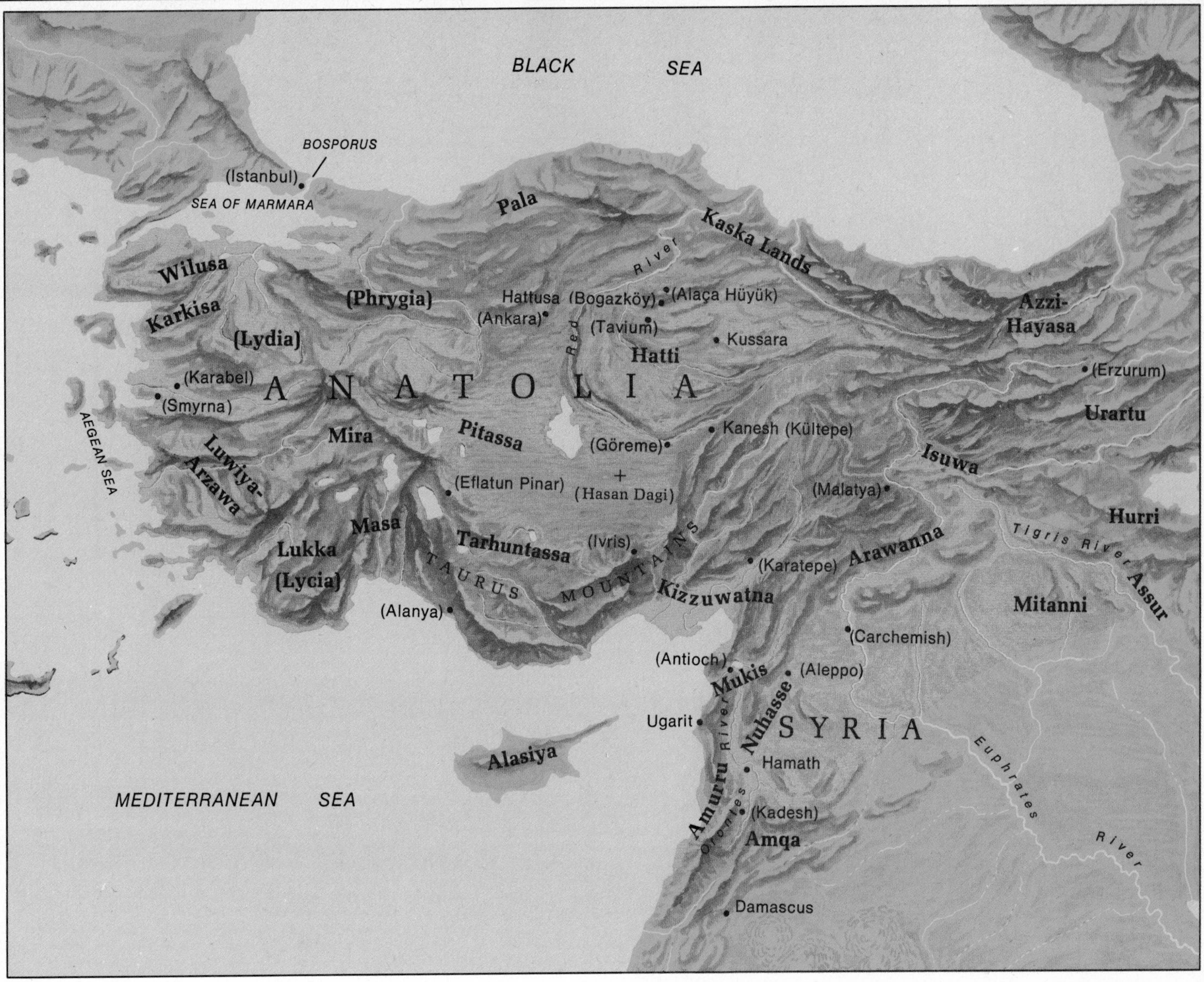

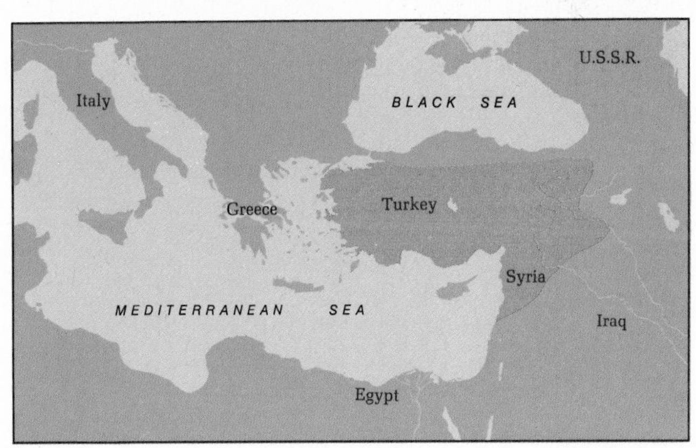

THE DOMAIN AT THE PEAK OF SUPREMACY

The rugged plateau of Anatolia, shown on this map of Asia Minor *(above)*, was the home of the Hittite Empire. Radiating in all directions from its birthplace, the land of Hatti, the empire expanded and contracted during its 500-year span. Its expanse at the height of power in the 14th Century B.C. is roughly indicated here by the brown area. The map includes names *(marked by dots)* of Hittite towns and archeological sites mentioned in this book, as well as the names of Hittite vassal states or bordering peoples *(boldface type)*. Modern or classical place names are set off in parentheses. The smaller map locates Asia Minor in relation to southern Europe and to Egypt, the Hittites' great rival.

glyphs. The name by which they became known —Hittites—is not actually their own but comes from Hatti, the older designation for the region they eventually made their homeland and base of empire.

The Hittites apparently had as cloudy a view of this formative period in their history as do scholars today. A Hittite scribe around 1700 B.C. copied a much earlier story of Pitkhana and his son, Anitta —two kings of an Anatolian city-state called Kussara. The scribe credited them with conquering a rival city named Nesa—also known as Kanesh, where the Assyrian merchants resided; a spearhead bearing Anitta's name was found there. But more important to the early history of the Hittites, Anitta also overcame Hattusa, at that time the capital of the country of Hatti. "I took it by storm in the night, and where it had been, I sowed weeds," the Hittite scribe has recorded Anitta as saying. "Whosoever becomes king after me and again settles Hattusa, may the Storm God of Heaven strike him."

While the spiritual heritage of Anitta was treasured in Hittite legend for centuries to come, his curse was ignored. The Hittites—doubtless recognizing the strategic position of Hattusa—rebuilt it around 1650 B.C. and made it their capital.

It is chiefly from the ruins of this fortress-like city —from rock carvings found there and at a nearby Hittite shrine called Yazilikaya ("inscribed rock" in Turkish) and from the great number of clay tablets recovered from long-buried royal archives—that archeologists and historians have learned the true nature of this long-obscure people. Even the most random sampling of these discoveries is enough to reestablish the fact that the Hittites were remarkable in a variety of ways, including their appearance, their behavior and their beliefs.

The rock carvings of mortals and of gods and goddesses apparently cast in the image of their worshipers give some idea of what the Hittites looked like and how they dressed. They are shown as short and broad-shouldered, with long, hooked noses and high, sloping foreheads. Some of the men sport beards without mustaches; those who are clean-shaven have receding chins. Because the men are often represented with pigtails, some early students of the Hittites concluded that they were of Mongolian extraction, basing this notion apparently on the Chinese queue and overlooking the fact that at various times in history Westerners also have worn pigtails.

The Hittite men are always portrayed with earrings and sometimes with high dome-shaped helmets or tight-fitting caps. Both men and women wear long woolen robes, although the males are occasionally dressed in a shorter belted tunic, sometimes with a long cloak over it. Many of the goddesses are clad in ankle-length pleated skirts bound at the waist by a broad belt, garments presumably worn by the high-ranking Hittite women also.

And almost always the Hittite men and women are shod in what came to be the most distinctive Hittite trademark: pointed boots, turned up at the toe and worn not only in their own mountainous terrain but even—if Egyptian sculptors of monuments can be believed—when they pushed into the plains of Syria to meet an Egyptian challenge.

Except for their distinctive boots, their clothes are not markedly different from those of their neighbors —perhaps another indication of the ease with which the Hittites adopted local ways. That they were in-

Two Contemporary Views of the Hittites

Two views of the Hittites—a bronze statue (rear and front aspects) and an Egyptian wall relief—present them at their peak and after their decline. The statue was cast between the 15th and 13th centuries B.C. when Hittite hegemony extended over most of Asia Minor; the long, thick pigtail, a Hittite affectation, may have been worn not merely as decoration but also as a neck guard in battle. The relief dates from the first half of the 12th Century B.C. when the great empire crumbled; the figure in the middle is a Hittite prisoner. His comrades-in-defeat are (from left), a Libyan, a Syrian, one of the Sea Peoples and a second Syrian.

An imaginative potter turned to the jaunty, curled-at-the-toes Hittite boot as the inspiration for a libation cup, used in 19th Century B.C. religious rituals. This type of footwear, characteristic of Hittite dress, is still worn in some parts of Turkey.

veterate mixers is unmistakably clear from the fact that no fewer than eight languages were used in the edicts, letters, treaties, laws, army orders and religious instructions unearthed at Hattusa. Among these languages were Akkadian, or Babylonian, which had become the lingua franca of the ancient world and which the Hittites employed extensively for diplomatic correspondence with Egypt and other foreign realms; Hattic, the language of the original inhabitants of the land and called Hattili by Hittites; the official language, the Indo-European tongue known today as Hittite and which the Hittites themselves seem to have called Nesite (after the city of Nesa conquered by the early kings of Kussara); a poorly documented tongue called Palaic; and Luwian, the language of the Indo-European-speaking people who may have preceded the Hittites into Asia Minor.

Not all these languages were of equal importance or currency, and Hittite scribes, to avoid confusing their own countrymen—and only incidentally to ease the tortuous path of translation for modern interpreters—would announce, before throwing a bit of, say, Luwian into the text, "What follows is in Luwian."

As centuries passed, the Hittite trademark—the elfin boots depicted in the rock carvings—and the fierce, stocky men who displayed it became familiar sights throughout the Near East. All too familiar to some of their military opponents. The Egyptians, who referred to the Hittite kingdom as Hatti, at times called it "abominable Hatti," an appellation that, considering the rivalry between the two empires, was in its own way complimentary.

There is no doubt that the Hittites were highly aggressive or that they could fight well; their battle tactics were brilliant and the military vehicle they are thought to have developed—the light, fast, three-man chariot (one man to drive and two to do combat) —was a splendidly successful machine. But for that era, when sometimes whole populations were slaughtered or enslaved, the Hittites appear to have been unusually humane.

The Hittite sovereigns often welcomed surrendering princes into vassalage and bound the peace package with treaties and written oaths, at times sealing the deal with a royal marriage (there seems to have been a plenitude of Hittite princesses available for this purpose). They ran most of their empire by a system that allowed their vassal states as much freedom as possible, short of letting them control their own foreign policies.

So constituted, the Hittite Empire was something quite new in the ancient world; Egyptians often used governors and physical occupation to rule their conquests. Nonetheless, the unique Hittite system had its drawbacks. As one eminent Hittitologist, Professor O. R. Gurney of Oxford, points out, it "created a brittle structure. When a Hittite king died, the vassals tended to break away and had to be reunited by the next king—if he could do it."

The legalistic base of their empire reflected the Hittites' deep respect for law. For example, official instructions given to the commandants of border guards, who had some judicial responsibilities in their districts, clearly spelled out a principle of justice that would be welcomed as progress if applied in many parts of the world today:

"He must not decide [the case in hand] in favor of his superior, he must not decide it in favor of his brother, his wife, or his friend; no one shall be

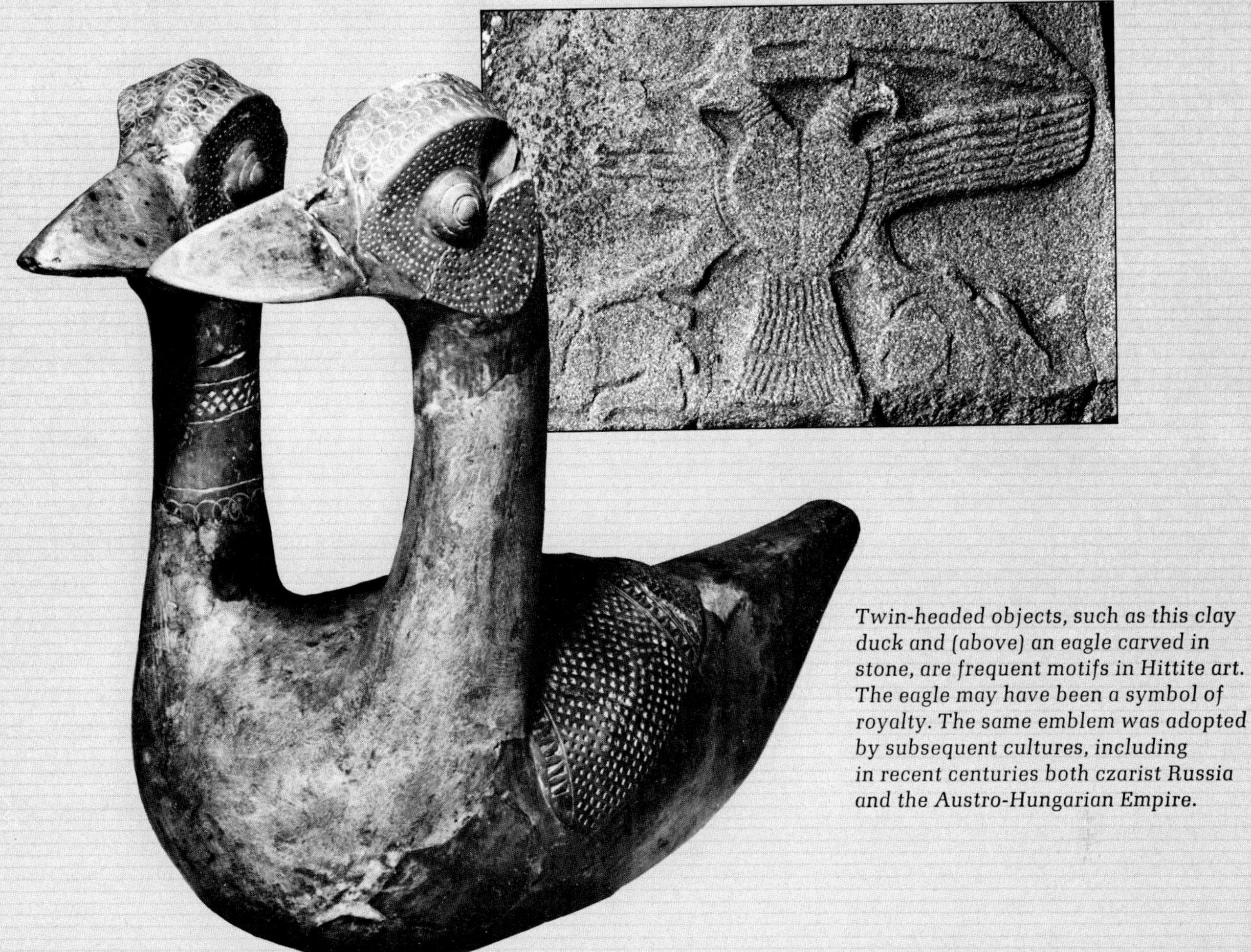

Twin-headed objects, such as this clay duck and (above) an eagle carved in stone, are frequent motifs in Hittite art. The eagle may have been a symbol of royalty. The same emblem was adopted by subsequent cultures, including in recent centuries both czarist Russia and the Austro-Hungarian Empire.

shown any favor. He must not make a just case unjust; he must not make an unjust case just. Whatever is right, that shall he do."

The Hittite king himself, especially in the earlier stages of empire building, was subject to law in a way that has led some writers to call the Hittite state the first known constitutional monarchy. An assembly known as the *pankus,* probably composed of nobles, sat in judgment of the king, warning him if he seemed about to infringe on the laws and having the power to execute him if he persisted.

The authority of the *pankus* waned as the empire grew and eventually seems to have vanished altogether. Some scholars cite this circumstance as evidence that the assembly was an institution that the Hittites brought with them into Asia Minor, where it gradually crumbled as the nation became increasingly Orientalized and Hittite monarchs took on the absolute character of their Egyptian and Near Eastern neighbors. A theory has been advanced—but not proved—that originally the *pankus* elected the king as "first among equals," a view that if correct could be highly enlightening. Since it is known that some early Germanic societies, including the Anglo-Saxons, elected their monarchs, the possibility that the Hittites also did so presents one of those tantalizing, half-open windows into the past through which historians, if only they could fling it wide, might learn something important about the early growth and spread of political structures and the early movement of European peoples.

For all their political sophistication the Hittites were firm believers in the efficacy of curses in reinforcing their international dealings. Their treaties with foreign powers not only contained extensive oaths and long lists of gods who were called on to wit-

Remnants of the once-grand Hittite capital of Hattusa—a city as large as ancient Athens—strew rocky hillsides. The masonry visible on the terrace

(right of center) is all that survives of the Great Temple; crumbling stone walls on top of the crag (left of temple) mark the site of the royal palace.

ness them, but also incorporated specific curses that were supposed to go into effect automatically, like buried land mines, should anyone break his word. In ingenuity of cursing, some Hittite rulers rose to artistry: "May the gods blot you out. May the earth be ice so that you fall down slipping. May the soil of your country be a hardened quagmire so that you break in, but never get across."

The Hittites were as passionate about serving their gods as they were about calling them down upon the heads of others. Their religious calendar was a compulsive force that superseded almost all else. Hittite kings were forever rushing back from the battlefield, leaving an unfinished campaign in the hands of a general, to fulfill their ritual duties as primates of the national faith.

Nothing, however, characterized the Hittites' religious beliefs so much as tolerance, a quality that must have enhanced their ability to enlist the loyalty of nations they conquered. When Hittites absorbed an alien people, they absorbed that people's gods as well, adding new deities willy-nilly to their crowded pantheon. Moreover, the maintenance of the newcomer's shrines was an order of highest priority for the local governor and military commander. In fact, it would appear that all but a few of the Hittites' gods were borrowed from other peoples after the Hittites reached Asia Minor.

Hittite culture (using the word in its narrowest sense, to mean the arts) has been found wanting by some scholars when compared with the artistic achievements of their contemporaries—the Egyptians, the Babylonians and other neighboring civilized societies —particularly for its lack of dynamic development.

A Hittite Chronology

c. 2000 B.C.
Moving down from their original home somewhere in Europe (possibly southwestern Russia), the Hittites, a people of Indo-European stock, settle in Asia Minor.

c. 1900 B.C.
Scribes at an Assyrian trading post in the city of Kanesh make the first written references to Hittites, thus providing the earliest proof of the newcomers' presence in Anatolia.

c. 1900 B.C.
King Anitta of Kussara conquers rival city-states, including Hattusa, future capital of the Hittite Empire.

c. 1680-1650 B.C.
Labarna I sets about uniting rival city-states.

c. 1650-1620 B.C.
Labarna II continues expansion of the kingdom, establishes his capital at Hattusa and changes his name to Hattusili I: "man of Hattusa."

c. 1600 B.C.
Mursili I sacks Babylon.

1590-1560 B.C.
Territory is lost in the south and power struggles disrupt royal leadership.

1525-1500 B.C.
Telipinu establishes hereditary law of succession. He is the first Hittite king to make a treaty with a foreign power; also the last ruler of the Old Kingdom.

c. 1386-1348 B.C.
King Suppiluliuma I extends Hittite hegemony over most of Asia Minor, as far south as present-day Damascus and east beyond the Euphrates. The empire begins.

c. 1300 B.C.
Cold war with Egypt erupts into the Battle of Kadesh.

c. 1200 B.C.
Hittite Empire comes to an abrupt end.

709 B.C.
Neo-Hittites, who kept remnants of Hittite culture alive, succumb to Assyrian hegemony.

The surviving examples of Hittite visual art—mainly statuettes in stone or bronze, seal impressions and rock carvings—have been criticized for owing more to boldness than to perfection.

Minor though their art may have been, the Hittites did preserve and bequeath to the world one very ancient Near Eastern motif—the double-headed eagle that crops up frequently in their rock carvings. Byzantine emperors took over the emblem, as did the Seljuk Turks who dominated Anatolia 2,000 years after the Hittites. In the modern era both Austria and czarist Russia adopted it for their national symbols.

Hittite written literature, too, has been given low grades, although there may have been a great oral tradition. Samples found so far consist mainly of myths, legends and hymns, and include no great epics. The literature does, however, display flashes of humor and emotional warmth unusual in the writings of that early age. Consider, for example, the myth of the god Telipinu. Angry, for some reason that must remain unknown unless the missing fragments of the clay tablet turn up, Telipinu became so agitated that he shouted, "There must be no interference!" and then "tried to put his right shoe on his left foot and his left shoe on his right foot." This incisive description of rage and frustration, born in the brain of some long-dead Hittite scribe or storyteller, easily leaps the gulf of time between his era and our own—human imagination touching human imagination across the 35 intervening centuries.

And no modern father's advice to his son shows more wary understanding of a young man's inclination to plunge into life's pitfalls than that of a Hittite king named Hattusili. In a speech recorded about 1620 B.C., he told his newly adopted son and heir to "keep thy father's word" and stay away from wine in favor of bread and water while a youth, but when "old age is within thee, then drink to satiety! And then thou mayest set aside thy father's word." Here is a man speaking in a tongue now so dead that the most learned philologists do not know exactly how he pronounced the words. Yet he conveys such intelligent perception as to make a 20th Century audience regret all the more that information about the Hittites is still so incomplete.

In addition to the already-mentioned holes in that knowledge—their origin, the course of their movement into Asia Minor, details of their early days in Anatolia—there are also tantalizing gaps in their social history. The records discovered thus far are chiefly royal edicts and writings dealing with matters of state. The buildings that have been exhumed and studied are mainly palaces, administrative centers and temples. As for how life was lived by the great bulk of the common people, we know little; there are no surviving private letters or contracts between businessmen and only a few "everyday" artifacts. Historians know how the monarch ran his household, down to the detail that royal water carriers were ordered to strain his water (one, named Zuliya, failed to do so and was executed when his majesty found a hair in the pitcher); but in many instances they can only theorize about how a farm wife in the valley below the palace ran hers.

Even their official history—the stories of their kings and wars—raises more questions than existing records can answer. The most frustrating question of all is—what happened to the Hittites? After half a millennium of vigorous and influential existence, their civilization seems to have come to an abrupt

Viewed from the steep slope on which the royal palace once stood, the foundation stones of the Great Temple, the largest of Hattusa's holy places,

dominate a panorama of the Anatolian plateau. The clustered, red-tiled rooftops to the left belong to the present-day Turkish town of Bogazköy.

end around 1200 B.C., slipping into the near-total oblivion that was to last for 3,000 years.

Until about a decade ago, certain tablets thought to date from the reigns of Tudhaliya IV and Arnuwanda III, who ruled during the last half century of the Hittite Empire, seemed to offer at least a partial explanation of the Hittites' fall. The tablets described a bitter struggle in western Asia Minor with a rebellious vassal prince named Madduwatta. Some historians supposed that this revolt must have spread and contributed heavily to the sudden disintegration of the once-mighty empire.

But now some Hittitologists have begun to reexamine and challenge the accepted dating of these and other Hittite texts, and thus of the events they mention. A team at the University of Chicago's Oriental Institute, under Professor H. G. Güterbock, enlisted the assistance of a computer. They fed it punch cards on which Hittite texts had been broken down in ways that enabled the computer to compare the texts for elements that might have changed with the passing of time—grammar, syntax, spelling.

There is certainly something incongruous about the notion of an ancient Hittite scribe bent over a clay tablet, marking with a stylus words that would one day appear as patterns of holes on a computer punch card. Nevertheless, the computer indicated enough changes to add new converts to the theory that the texts had been wrongly dated and belonged not to the 13th Century B.C. but to an earlier period of Hittite history. The results of this experiment have failed to convince all Hittitologists, however, and the case for redating the texts still is not strong enough to warrant rewriting Hittite history.

If the texts do indeed turn out to date back a century or more earlier than previously believed, some of the deeds until now attributed to Tudhaliya IV and Arnuwanda III will have to be repositioned in history. The struggle with the rebel vassal prince would have taken place at some earlier time, thereby extinguishing whatever light this revolt seemed to throw on the collapse of Hittite power.

The mysteries that still surround the Hittites could have been even deeper, the darkness more nearly total. The truth about them might never have become known at all had there not commenced, little more than a century ago, a chain reaction of chance finds, adventurous speculation, and hard-slogging research that led to an achievement unparalleled in archeology: the discovery of a lost empire.

Hattusa, Cradle and Bastion of Power

Perched on the rocky citadel (upper left), the palace of the Hittite kings looks down on fortifications and the Great Temple (far right).

To the Hittites of the 14th and 13th centuries B.C., their capital of Hattusa was far more than the command post of an expanding empire. It had been their home base since about 1650 B.C., and long habitation had made it the epitome of their culture and character. In sum, the city marked them as a superbly organized people with a genius for wielding political power.

In the 14th Century B.C., Hattusa grew phenomenally, in scale with the Hittite conquests of the time. The 160-acre old town doubled in size, expanding upslope on both sides of two broad valleys. To defend the enlarged urban complex, an immense labor force of enslaved war prisoners and drafted freemen built a prodigious extension of the old wall. Snaking across hills and valleys, the wall formed an enclosure that, in case of attack, was large enough to accommodate the entire population of the surrounding area. With the completion of this epic project, Hattusa stood as the largest, most strongly fortified city of its time.

Through the monumental Lion Gate, a chariot leaves the capital city with royal orders to be delivered to a distant garrison. The gateway, whose

parabolic arch is believed to be a Hittite invention, was flanked by two massive rectangular towers.

Walls, Chariots and the Long Arm of Imperial Rule

From almost every spot in Hattusa, citizens saw reassuring signs of the Hittites' military might. Powerful defenses—the capital's outer wall and interior bastions—loomed up everywhere, and well-trained soldiers stationed at the garrison in the citadel mounted guard at many critical points throughout the city.

Another martial sight—the frequent arrival and departure of war chariots at Hattusa's five main gates—constantly dramatized the imperial scope of Hittite power. The simple, efficient design of these chariots contributed enormously to Hittite victories on the battlefield: the vehicles were sturdy enough to carry, in addition to a skilled driver, a shield-bearer for defense as well as a spearman for attack.

Just as important, the chariot traffic to and from the capital kept the king in effective contact with the outposts of his far-flung empire. The Hittite rulers realized that they could not govern their many conquered peoples directly or by force alone, and so they pragmatically restored the defeated local rulers to limited power as vassals, guaranteeing them protection in return for a pledge of loyalty and support. But it was the implied threat of strong, strategically located garrisons—manned by Hittite troops and commanded by royal relatives or Hittite officers of proven loyalty—that held together the imperial patchwork of conquered realms.

Palace and Temple: Twin Cornerstones of the Realm

From his palace atop Hattusa's lofty citadel, the king saw spread out below him the buildings of the Great Temple, the religious center of the empire. The view from the heights was an impressive one—and symbolic as well. For the king was also the high priest of the land, and the national religion helped to shore up his secular rule by imparting a degree of cultural unity to the empire's diverse peoples.

Doubly powerful in their dual role, the Hittite kings could have suppressed the local deities in conquered territories—an abrasive policy at best. Instead, they adopted many foreign gods into the capacious Hittite pantheon. Indeed, most of the Hittite gods were borrowed, including even the supreme deity, Teshub, the Storm God, whose preeminence might well have been due to the winter gales and blizzards that battered the Hittites' rugged upland home.

Chief among the kings' religious duties was an annual tour of the empire's major shrines in order to celebrate important festivals on specific dates. Partly because public appearances helped to stabilize the realm and to bring in rich donations, the kings permitted nothing to stand in the way of their priestly itinerary. And so important did they regard their spiritual responsibilities in general that one king even left his army during a campaign to preside at a scheduled ceremony in Hattusa.

Transporting supplies, servants trudge the snowy slope of the citadel overlooking the Great Temple,

where the king served as both head of state and chief priest. This temple was the largest of five temples built in Hattusa during the imperial age.

In the Royal Hall: Homage to the Great King

High on Hattusa's citadel, in a huge room that occupied the entire second story of the royal palace, the political ties that connected the Hittite Empire were renewed each year in a solemn ceremony: the payment of homage and tribute to the Great King.

The time selected for the ritual is unknown. But by the scheduled date, delegations from all the imperial territories had converged on the capital. With each came a caravan laden with lavish gifts—gold bars and goblets, fine weapons and jewelry, purple cloth and perfumed oil.

Though uniformly rich in dress and tribute, the delegations varied significantly in status and composition. Of the 12 groups that paid annual homage to the greatest Hittite conqueror, King Suppiluliuma I (1386-1348 B.C.), two consisted of dignitaries representing protectorates—realms of special importance to which the king granted trade advantages and a degree of independence. While the rulers of the protectorates were allowed to pledge fealty by proxy, the princes of the 10 vassal states were required to appear in person before the king.

Of course vows of loyalty could be broken. Yet the compacts they sealed were soundly based on mutual duties and benefits: the princes got protection from the king, and the king got funds and troops from the princes. While this balance held, the Hittite Empire remained a prodigy of power.

Preparing to do homage in the palace's audience hall, envoys (foreground) from the Syrian city-state

of Ugarit show their lavish tribute to a Hittite official, while at left several delegations queue up in front of the king, enthroned in the background.

Chapter Two: Rediscovering the Hittites

How is it possible that a people as great as the Hittites could be completely forgotten? While the memory of their contemporaries, the Egyptians and Babylonians, lingered on, nothing of the Hittites seemed to survive except their name—and even that was misapplied. And yet there was one mention of them in the Bible that early 19th Century scholars could not reconcile with other Biblical references that made the Hittites seem nothing more than a minor group of tribesmen.

The reference is found in chapters six and seven of the Second Book of Kings. The king of Syria had marched his entire army to Samaria, capital of the Kingdom of Israel, and laid siege to the city. Inside its walls the defenders ran out of food and grew desperate. Finally, when they had been reduced to eating asses' heads and doves' dung, they were rescued by a miracle. The Lord "made the army of the Syrians hear the sounds of chariots and of horses, the sound of a great army." The terrified Syrians panicked, abandoned their tents and horses on the spot and fled for their lives, crying, "Behold, the king of Israel has hired against us the kings of the Hittites and the kings of Egypt to come upon us."

This allusion stuck in the academic throat. It implied that the Hittites were an awesome power deserving equal status with Egyptians as symbols of might and terror. In the middle of the 19th Century one distinguished scholar, voicing the opinion of most of his learned colleagues, concluded that so respectful a reference to "kings of the Hittites" must be incorrect and irrelevant. He dismissed the passage for its "unhistorical tone." And so the matter rested; the Hittites might as well never have existed.

The puzzling Biblical reference to them, as it is now understood by scholars, refers not to the Hittites of Hattusa, but to people who survived them after the collapse of the empire around 1200 B.C. Along with their predecessors' name, these so-called neo-Hittites apparently retained some reputation for military prowess. Nonetheless, had mid-19th Century scholars not been so closed-minded and had they looked beyond the Bible, they might have wakened to the fact that there was hard evidence—literally as hard as stone—of the Hittites' power. Some of that testimony already had been discovered and in places as widely separated as western Syria and northern Anatolia—clues, if anyone at the time had been able to read them, to the magnitude of the Hittite Empire.

The solution to the mystery of the Hittites properly begins in the 1830s with a French explorer wandering through the wilds of Anatolia. Unaware of the Hittites, he was searching for the ruins of Tavium, a settlement of Roman times.

In common with many adventurous men of his era, Charles-Félix-Marie Texier had been swept up in the then new and fashionable passion for archeology. Ever since exciting reports of temples, tombs and treasure had come back from Egypt in the wake of Napoleon's invasion, Europeans in ever-growing numbers—from serious students to acquisitive tourists—had been trampling over Egypt and other centers of ancient civilizations. In their digging, find-

The larger-than-life-sized figure of King Tudhaliya stands in a niche in a cliff in Karabel, Turkey. Carved more than 3,000 years ago, the relief had been seen by many travelers and noted by the Greek historian Herodotus; but it was not correctly identified until 1879, when British scholar A. H. Sayce pronounced its style—and the inscriptions—Hittite.

One of the earliest published views of the Hittite capital of Hattusa, this 19th Century French engraving shows the sprawling ruins of the Temple of the Storm God and the Sun Goddess. The engraving was made from an on-the-spot drawing by Hattusa's discoverer, Charles-Félix-Marie Texier.

ing, sketching and carting away of ancient artifacts, they often used methods that destroyed more historical information than was recovered.

Texier, with the backing of the French government, was delighted to receive permission from the Ottoman Turks to explore Asia Minor, the heart of their empire. Because the Turks were suspicious of Westerners, they had allowed few of them to travel there —a fact which certainly enhanced the preservation of the region's ruins and helped keep the secret of the Hittites. It also meant that Texier had few reports from earlier travelers to guide him. Regretting this scarcity of information, the Frenchman set off across Turkey's central plateau in July of 1834.

Whenever Texier encountered local inhabitants, he asked if there were old ruins in the neighborhood. At a village called Bogazköy, about 90 miles east of the present Turkish capital of Ankara, he was directed to the craggy hills above the village. Texier followed the directions and at the end of a tiring climb was stunned by what he beheld: huge blocks of stone that once formed the foundations of a large building; the remains of a towered wall fortifying an area at least three-quarters of a mile across and with a perimeter of four miles; and two gateways, one guarded by stone lions and another bearing a larger-than-life carving of a man, possibly a king.

As he was marveling at the magnificence and extent of the ruins, never dreaming that they belonged to the splendid Hittite capital of Hattusa, he was told by one of the villagers of another place that might interest him—Yazilikaya. After a mile-long hike over a narrow, twisting path, Texier again found himself forgetting his fatigue in the excitement of discovery.

At Yazilikaya deep crevices in the limestone created what appeared to be a sanctuary consisting of a pair of grassy alcoves connected by clefts in the rock. It was not the natural beauty of the place that took away Texier's breath, however, but the handiwork of long-dead men *(page 35)*.

The walls of the larger alcove were covered with rock carvings that were both impressive and strange: a parade of godlike figures, some wearing conical helmets, others in crownlike headgear. Some stood balanced on the backs of animals, some on the shoulders of figures who may have represented other gods. Some were winged. Several of the figures carried mysterious objects in their hands.

On one wall of the smaller alcove 12 identical gods or warriors, bearing swords, strode across the rock face single file, frozen for millennia in their martial lock step. On the opposite wall a giant figure extended one arm before him and protectively wrapped the other about the shoulders of a much smaller man. And in several places the bas-reliefs were embellished with groups of enigmatic hieroglyph-like symbols. Some were recognizable shapes: headless bodies, a hand, animal heads and a mountain. Others were abstract, geometric forms—lines, rectangles, arcs and circles—combined in various ways.

Neither the style of the artists, the dress of the figures nor the mysterious symbols accompanying them resembled those of any ancient culture within Texier's knowledge. He was certain that they and the ruins nearby could not be the remains of Tavium. "No edifice of any Roman era could be fitted in here," he wrote. "The grandeur and the peculiar nature of the ruins perplexed me extraordinarily when I attempted to give the city its historical name."

One conclusion, however, was strikingly apparent:

the city that had crowned this rugged terrain was no insignificant place and could have been erected by no insignificant tribe. Its size, the massiveness of the stones used in its buildings, and the amount and substance of its art proclaimed the work of a rich, powerful and ambitious people.

When Texier's book on his explorations in Asia Minor appeared in 1839, his discovery did not shake the scholarly world. A great nation that left remains like those he described simply did not fit into the structure of ancient history as it then existed; and historians of the day, reluctant to upset that structure, regarded Texier's finds almost as a nuisance. They would have been even more disquieted had they realized that his discovery was linked to an earlier one made more than 350 miles south of his ruined city.

The earlier find, which had been reported—and ignored—12 years before the Frenchman began his Anatolian explorations, was the work of a man with an extraordinary craving for travel and adventure. Swiss-born and German-educated, Johann Ludwig Burckhardt *(page 37)* found a way, in England, to satisfy his interests through the Association for Promoting the Discovery of the Interior Parts of Africa. A privately financed society, the association was devoted to advancing geographical knowledge and, not incidentally, to expanding the borders of the British Empire. Burckhardt was given an amazing assignment: to make his way across the Sahara to West Africa and to find the source of the Niger River.

After a quick course in Arabic, he left England in 1809 bound for Syria, where he intended to master the language. In order not to arouse suspicion as a Westerner and to help explain his foreign accent, he assumed the guise of Sheik Ibrahim, a Moslem trader from distant India. After nearly three years in Syria, he not only spoke Arabic fluently but had also become an expert in Islamic law.

Political disturbances that prevented caravans from crossing the Sahara frustrated his search for the Niger's source, so Burckhardt spent another five years traveling through Syria, Palestine, Egypt, Nubia, Abyssinia and the Arabian peninsula. Through his intimate knowledge of Islamic law he even won permission to make a pilgrimage to the sacred city of Mecca; he was the first European ever to do so.

Still waiting for his opportunity to cross the desert to western Africa, Burckhardt died of dysentery in Cairo in 1817. He had written detailed journals of his travels, however, and the diaries were printed posthumously in England.

In one journal, published in 1822, Burckhardt mentioned an odd stone he had come across in the Syrian city of Hamath (modern Hama). It was fixed in the corner of a house and was covered with what looked like hieroglyphs. Burckhardt was familiar with Egyptian hieroglyphs, but these were markedly different.

Although everybody with an interest in the Near East avidly read his books, and although his truthfulness and accuracy were widely acknowledged, no one perceived any significance in Burckhardt's find. Not until 1870 was the stone rediscovered. Two Americans—J. Augustus Johnson, the United States consul general in Syria, and a missionary named Jessup—found not only Burckhardt's stone but three more like it, covered with hieroglyphs, located in odd places around the town. They also learned that the people of Hamath had a fierce reverence for these stones. Among other things, the inhabitants apparently believed the mysterious inscriptions were a magical cure for rheumatism.

"We did not succeed in getting . . . impressions," Johnson said, "for fanatical Moslems crowded upon us when we began to work upon the stones, and we were obliged to be content with such copies . . . as could be obtained by the aid of a native painter."

When Johnson published one of the imperfect paintings of the stones in a scholarly quarterly the following year, the stones suddenly became an alluring new honeypot for the antiquarian bees who were by now swarming over the Near East. Almost at once several other attempts were made to get impressions, tracings or photographs of the stones, but they met with little success.

In Damascus an Irish missionary named William Wright, who had an archeological bent, observed the developing situation with some anxiety. Soon, he wrote, "a new and altogether different set of men began to bully and barter for the coveted curiosities." A "very large sum of money" was offered for one of the stones, but the people of Hamath refused to sell. Wright feared the "fussy peddling" might result in the destruction of the stones. He determined to save them—or at least to make accurate copies.

His chance came late in 1872 when he and W. Kirby Green, the British consul at Damascus, were invited to join Syria's Turkish governor, Subhi Pasha, on an official visit to Hamath. When told about the stones, the urbane governor, who happened to be a patron of the Istanbul Archeological Museum, readily agreed to help Wright get copies of them.

On their first morning in Hamath, a city of winding, narrow streets, Wright and Green set out to locate the stones. The task, the missionary said, "was not so easy as it might seem, for all whom we asked about them looked us steadily in the face and swore vehemently that there were no stones such as we sought in Hamath." Wright and Green might have despaired of ever finding them had they not decided to ask every person they met "in the hope that we might

The 19th Century Swiss explorer Johann Ludwig Burckhardt—shown with his discovery, the Hamath stone—traveled disguised as an Arab. Though he did not recognize the stone's hieroglyphs as Hittite, he described his find in an 1822 book, and thus became the first to offer evidence of the mysterious Hittites.

find someone not up to the plot of concealing the inscriptions from us."

But soon they encountered a man who owned a house in the wall of which one of the stones was embedded. With the conspiracy of silence broken, "we had no difficulty in finding all the stones," said Wright. Later that day they showed the inscriptions to Subhi Pasha. He immediately recognized the stones' importance and ordered that they be cut from the walls. In the meantime, he sent a telegram to the sultan asking him to accept the stones for the museum's collection.

This news brought sullen knots of Hamathites into the streets, muttering vows to destroy the inscriptions before they could be taken away. At Wright's suggestion, the governor posted soldiers to guard the stones until removal began the next day. After what Wright described as "an anxious and sleepless night," work began early in the morning and "kept the city in an uproar" all day long. Two of the stones had to be extracted from the walls of inhabited houses. One was so gargantuan that 50 men and four oxen struggled the entire day to haul it the one mile to the government guesthouse, where Wright and Green were staying as the guests of Subhi Pasha. By evening the four inscribed blocks were secured there to protect them from the city's inhabitants. But the crisis was not over.

That night Hamath witnessed a spectacular meteor shower and "beheld in every brilliant sparkling train the wrath of heaven." Through the streets ran shouting men invoking the names of Allah and Mohammed and proclaiming the astral display to be an evil omen. In the morning a solemn delegation of Hamath's citizens called on Subhi Pasha, urging him to replace the stones to prevent the calamity prophesied by the skies. The governor gravely asked if anyone had been injured by the falling stars.

When it was agreed that no one had been hurt, the governor switched his mood to one of cheerful confidence. "Ah," he said, or so Wright related, "the omens were good. They indicated the shining approbation of Allah on your loyalty in sending these precious stones to your beloved Khalif, the Father of the Faithful." Comforted by this wisdom, the deputation withdrew.

Wright was still resolved to make plaster casts of the inscriptions. It was a long way to the Istanbul Archeological Museum and "we knew not what might happen to the stones." He and the British consul Kirby Green spent the next two days scrubbing them clean of builders' mortar and the moss and dirt that for centuries had been accumulating in the spaces between the raised characters.

Unable to find any plaster of Paris in Hamath, they made their own, burning and pounding raw gypsum brought in from the countryside. According to Wright, the amiable Turkish governor frequently invited them to leave their work to "shoot woodcock, or to hunt wild boars, or to stalk gazelles and bustards; but we stuck to our task until we had two perfect plaster casts of all the inscriptions."

One set was dispatched to the British Museum, the other to the Palestine Exploration Fund. Now scholars had access to these ancient, puzzling inscriptions, but it remained to be learned what the strange characters meant—and what people had written them. Wright, a firm believer in the Bible's validity as a basic historical document, built much of his speculation on the Biblical references to the Hittites, and with these in mind, thought he had an answer to the second question. As he later wrote, even before casts were made of the stones he had told the governor "that such inscriptions . . . would show that a great people, called Hittites in the Bible, but never referred to in classic history, had once formed a mighty empire in that region."

If there were scholars who became aware of the Irish missionary's guess, however, they must have brushed it off as wild and unlikely. The indecipherable writing on the stones became known as "Hamathite," for the place of its discovery.

It soon developed that the stones of Hamath were not unique. Another stone bearing the mysterious Hamathite hieroglyphs had been found at Aleppo, 75 miles north of Hamath. It was worn almost smooth because Moslems, believing it could cure not rheumatism but ophthalmia, had been rubbing it for centuries. But the people of Aleppo smashed the monument before accurate copies of the inscriptions could be made, confirming that Wright's suggestions for posting armed guards over the Hamath stones had been well founded.

Soon Hamathite was being found in the most unexpected places. In 1875 the Reverend E. J. Davis—Victorian clerics seem to have been particularly susceptible to archeology fever—visited a rock carving near Ivris in south-central Turkey. Long known but never properly copied, the bas-relief showed two figures: a large god, wearing a conical helmet and turned-up boots, and facing him a smaller figure, a man with arms lifted in an attitude of worship. Davis found that the carving included several lines of strange symbols—which turned out to be Hamathite.

Not long after that, a British Museum expedition —believing (correctly) that it had found the site of Carchemish, an important trade center of antiquity —began digging on the upper Euphrates River at the Syrian-Turkish border. In short order more Hamathite inscriptions were unearthed.

Strangely, no one during this span linked any of the hieroglyphs with those that the French explorer Texier had discovered in 1834 on the rock carvings near Bogazköy in northern Anatolia, although other travelers since had visited the ruins and provided more detailed descriptions of the Texier rock carvings. A French professor named Georges Perrot had even published his photographs of some of the inscriptions in 1872 (that young invention, the camera, was proving a boon to archeologists; Wright bemoaned not having one at Hamath). The photographs eventually enabled a brilliant young Briton, Archibald Henry Sayce, to establish a link between the inscriptions Texier had come upon at Bogazköy and those being found elsewhere, and thus to arouse historians to the true significance of the stones.

At the age of 30, Sayce was already one of Britain's foremost philologists. He could write fluently in nearly two dozen ancient and modern languages (he had begun reading Homeric Greek at the age of 10) and was well known for his work on Sumerian and Assyrian grammars. He was also a gifted popularizer of even the most esoteric aspects of his studies and was much in demand as a public lecturer. In 1879, while examining Perrot's photographs, Sayce recognized that two or three of the hieroglyphs pictured "were identical with those on the stones of Hamath and Carchemish." They also bore a resemblance to pictures he had seen of "Egyptian" hieroglyphs, first reported by the ancient Greek historian Herodotus as accompanying rock carvings on a cliff near Smyrna on Turkey's Aegean coast—carvings that Herodotus had attributed to a pharaoh.

"Suddenly," wrote Sayce, "the truth flashed upon me." Within a few months he was scrambling up that same cliff to reassure himself by taking a first-hand look at the inscriptions. To protect him from the bandits who infested the area, 30 Turkish soldiers waited below while Sayce crouched in a niche of the cliff face making impressions of the hieroglyphs. He was already sure that Herodotus was wrong, that the carvings were not Egyptian but Hamathite.

Similar inscriptions had now been found from Anatolia to Syria, and from the western coast of Turkey to the upper reaches of the Euphrates. To Sayce, the use of a common script over this broad area implied the existence of a common culture, perhaps a common nationhood. Even before journeying to see the carvings near Smyrna, he had tentatively advanced this idea, but most of those who listened to him ridiculed such a history-shattering theory. On his return from Turkey in 1879, bearing copies of the Hamathite cliff inscriptions as additional supporting evidence, he restated his theory.

It was not until the following year that Sayce's views finally received enough publicity to compel wide attention. But by now he was convinced that he was right on several counts. Not only did the widespread distribution of Hamathite inscriptions on stones found far beyond Hamath suggest a powerful people occupying a large area, but Egyptian and Assyrian writings had recently come to light referring to a great people inhabiting a land called Hatti. In a brilliant leap of intuition, he contended that these

Kaiser Wilhelm II, in light suit (center), inspects a 1911 dig on the then Turkish-owned island of Corfu. Aggressively fostering Turkish-German relations, he made frequent visits to Turkey and even bought a vacation palace on Corfu. In gratitude for his pro-Turkish stand, the Turkish government had awarded German archeologists the right to excavate the Hittite ruins at Bogazköy and other newly discovered Hittite sites.

people were the Hittites of the Bible who, in the Second Book of Kings, joined forces with the Egyptians and descended upon the army of the Syrians. In a speech before a packed meeting of the Society for Biblical Archaeology in London, in 1880, Sayce came right out and said it—that the so-called Hamathite inscriptions were actually the work of an ancient people whose strength and extent had been tremendously underrated: the Hittites.

No doubt poor William Wright, the Irish missionary who had rescued the Hamath stones, would have been grateful to receive even the adverse criticism that greeted Sayce's theory. Wright had been saying the same thing for years without stirring up any debate at all. In 1874, only two years after salvaging the Hamath stones, Wright had published an article in the *British and Foreign Evangelical Review* saying that the Hamathite inscriptions were Hittite. When Wright's earlier publication was brought to Sayce's attention, he acknowledged its premise but insisted he had never heard of it until arriving at the idea on his own. Wright's conclusion, he said, had been "buried in the pages of a periodical better known to theologians than to Orientalists." Or perhaps the missionary's identification of the hieroglyphs as Hittite had been lost amid the welter of theories that had been proposed to explain their origin. One hypothesis contended that the signs were not writing at all but mere "vagaries of ornamentation"; another supported a connection with ancient Peru; still others attempted to link the symbols with Aztec, Japanese and Korean writing.

Despite Wright's claims, Sayce received the initial glory for rediscovering this forgotten people—or what there was of praise amid the catcalls; in some academic quarters he was known as the "inventor" of the Hittites. But rivalry did not prevent Wright and Sayce from exchanging information and working together. In 1884 Wright published the first book on the subject, *The Empire of the Hittites.*

Possibly recalling the lack of impact that his assertion of a decade earlier had had, Wright this time rejected timidity and scholarly reserve. "The object of this book," he said boldly in his very first sentence, "is to restore the Empire of the Hittites to its rightful position in secular history."

One extraordinary bit of evidence in support of Wright's thesis—albeit circumstantial—had been uncovered only after the main body of his book was already set in type. Wright managed to include it in his preface in the form of a letter from Sayce. Sayce had been examining the Egyptian monument at Thebes. It described in bas-reliefs the battle of Kadesh, in which the Egyptians faced a people they called the Hatti. While a number of European travelers had seen this tableau, none had ever noted, as Sayce did, that many of the Hatti warriors wore boots turned up at the toes—the same kind of boots depicted in rock carvings at distant Anatolia.

No matter how wild some of Wright's guesses, or how strained his logic in support of them, *The Empire of the Hittites* gave the established view of the past a jolt that cleared the way for a new branch of study, Hittitology. Man's perspective on ancient history would never be the same again.

Eventually Wright and Sayce were proved wrong in many particulars. But in the years following publication of *The Empire of the Hittites* their basic conclusions were supported by growing evidence. Some of it was uncovered by scientific diligence, some by accidents of the sort that had already produced much of what was known about the Hittites.

One of these chance finds was a discovery of enormous significance because of the light it shed not only on the Hittites but on the Egyptian Empire and on the interrelationship of the two. In 1887 near Tell el-Amarna, a village some 200 miles up the Nile from Cairo, an Egyptian woman found a trove of hundreds of inscribed clay tablets. One widely recounted but probably apocryphal version of her discovery suggests that she stumbled upon them while searching the ground for something to hurl at a party of trespassing foreign tourists. More reliable accounts have it that she ran across a chamber full of the tablets as she routinely scavenged the ruins of an ancient Egyptian city in search of building bricks. Believing the tablets to be useless bits of old clay, she sold them to a neighbor for what today would be the equivalent of about 50 cents. The buyer tossed them randomly into sacks and transported them by donkey-back to a nearby town, where he in turn sold them at bargain prices to native dealers in antiquities.

The dealers did not realize exactly what they had; indeed, they did not even know whether the tablets were genuine relics or forgeries. For one thing, the inscriptions on them were in wedge-shaped characters, a form of writing very different from the familiar pictorial hieroglyphs of Egypt. Through careless handling, many of the tablets that had survived for more than 3,000 years were destroyed, but some eventually reached Luxor, where they were seen by E. A. Wallis Budge, a representative of the British Museum. At first Budge was puzzled; he later wrote, "In shape and form, colour and material, the tablets were unlike any I had ever seen." Fortunately, however, Budge was acquainted with cuneiform. If he had not, he said, "I should certainly have rejected them as forgeries." After hours of painstaking study he decided that almost all the tablets were letters, many of them addressed to kings of Egypt. "I felt certain," he said, "that the tablets were both genuine and of very great historical importance."

They were indeed. The tablets that Budge salvaged for the British Museum and those that ultimately came into the possession of other museums and private collections had once formed part of the royal archives of Akhenaton, the 14th Century B.C. pharaoh who attempted to revolutionize Egypt's religion by replacing its many gods with the monotheistic worship of the Sun God. The letters included diplomatic correspondence with vassals and foreign powers, discussions about international trade, descriptions of gifts from vassals and complaints that the gifts sent to the writers were not valuable enough. When eventually they had been translated, the Tell el-Amarna letters, as they came to be called, had the effect of an electric light being switched on in a long-dark basement of history.

For Hittitologists, the tablets were a godsend. Archibald Henry Sayce did not hesitate to call them "next to the historical book of the Old Testament the most valuable record which the ancient civilised world of the East has bequeathed to us." Most of the Tell el-Amarna letters were written in Akkadian, the Babylonian tongue that was used for diplomatic correspondence throughout the ancient world. They presented a picture of the great Egyptian Empire crumbling at the edges as Akhenaton devoted himself almost entirely to his new, heretical religion. And, as was proved by the record of repeated entreaties for reinforcements from hard-pressed Eygptian commanders in Syria, the greatest threat was that of a rival power that was steadily encroaching southward—the Hittites. Furthermore, among the letters was one from a Hittite monarch congratulating Akhenaton on ascending the throne of Eygpt in 1375 B.C. That single document provided both the king's name—Suppiluliuma—and the first known date that could be ascribed unequivocally to a Hittite king.

Two of the Amarna letters, although written in the same cuneiform as the others, were not in Akkadian but in a completely unknown language. Since the correspondence was to and from a king of Arzawa (subsequently established as a Hittite vassal state), the language was given that name. In 1893 a French archeologist, Ernest Chantre, during a desultory excavation in the ruined city at Bogazköy in the Anatolian highlands, came upon two small fragments of cuneiform tablets in an indecipherable tongue. It turned out to be the same peculiar language of Arzawa—which, as time would show, was actually the Hittite tongue.

At the end of the 19th Century the most stunning discoveries about the Hittites were still to come. The existence of an extensive Hittite empire was by then widely conceded, but its shape and nature would remain grossly misunderstood as long as the Hittite language was beyond the grasp of the scholars.

Hittitologists, piecing together the finds made so far and, reinterpreting the Biblical accounts, conceived of a people who had pushed south, north and west from a Syrian homeland. Sayce was of the opinion that the earliest Hittites had descended originally from the snow-clad Taurus Mountains of southern Turkey—mainly because their upturned boots looked like snowshoes—but he surmised that their development as a powerful nation took place in Syria, that Carchemish had been their capital and that the ruins of Hattusa in central Anatolia marked the far northern fringe of their dominion.

In retrospect, it seems remarkable that those impressive remains, discovered by Texier in 1834 on the hills above Bogazköy, for so long escaped serious investigation by archeologists. As early as 1883 Sayce had urged Heinrich Schliemann, the discoverer of Troy, to dig at Bogazköy, but the great German-born excavator was busy with other projects. Ernest Chantre's digging there during 1893 had done little more than scratch the surface, as later work would dramatically demonstrate.

Not until the present century did the ruins of Hattusa at Bogazköy at last attract major archeological attention. And because of conditions far removed from scientific research—international politics—the fabulous secrets buried there were to be uncovered not by the British, who up to then had led in the rediscovery of the Hittites, but by the Germans.

In 1905 John Garstang, a British archeologist, had applied to the Ottoman Turks for permission to dig at Bogazköy. But the influence of Kaiser Wilhelm II was then paramount in Turkey *(page 40)*; a few years earlier the Deutsche Bank had undertaken construction of the Berlin-to-Baghdad railway, a project of immense economic importance to the Turks. While Garstang was raising funds for his expedition, Hugo Winckler, a German Assyriologist, had also applied for a permit to excavate the same site and had managed to enlist the support of the Kaiser, who wanted to balance his militaristic image with that of a patron of the arts and sciences. When the Kaiser's interest was made known to the sultan of Turkey, Hugo Winckler—not Garstang—won the concession to excavate at Bogazköy.

Winckler was a specialist in ancient languages, not an archeologist, and his unsystematic digging methods led Sayce to describe his receipt of the concession as "archeologically unfortunate." But while Winckler's methods drew valid complaints, his results were absolutely spectacular. His first expedition, in October 1905, was cut short after only three days by the early advent of heavy seasonal rains, but even in that brief period Winckler had recovered some 30 fragments of clay tablets. And he had pinpointed the exact area where he would dig the following year.

Returning in July 1906, he learned that summer on the Anatolian plateau was in some respects as disagreeable as the wet season. At midday, he said, the temperature "would have been not uncomfortable in a Turkish bath," and as soon as the sun set, a bone-chilling wind howled down from the mountains. Despite the intense heat, Winckler was compelled to work with head and neck covered, and with gloved hands even when copying tablets, to protect himself from swarms of stinging flies.

No amount of physical discomfort, however, could diminish his increasing excitement about what his workmen's spades were revealing. Almost as soon as they resumed digging where most of the previous year's finds had been made, the men began pulling out tablets and fragments of tablets by dozens, then by scores, and finally at the rate of 100 to 200 a day.

"That it had been a great center was now quite clear," Winckler wrote, "and that it could not be the remains of the archives of an insignificant king ... was also definite." Most of the tablets were in the still untranslatable Arzawa language first found at Tell el-Amarna. But soon some pieces in Akkadian, the readable tongue of the Babylonians, emerged —bits of correspondence between two kings, one an Egyptian, the other a king of the Hittites.

Thus, within a few days of starting to dig no doubt remained in Winckler's mind that he was excavating the capital of the Hittite Empire and that he had unearthed the royal archives of Hittite kings who had been in contact with the pharaohs of Egypt. The find would make headlines and remake history. The first glow of elation he experienced, however, was soon eclipsed by a further and even more astonishing discovery, one for which he "had not dared to hope."

On August 20, 1906, as Winckler sat swathed in his stifling protective clothing, swatting at flies and furiously copying cuneiform inscriptions from tablets that were piling up faster than he could handle them, an assistant brought him a particularly splendid specimen that had just been uncovered.

"One look at it," Winckler said, "and all the experiences of my life paled into insignificance." He was already familiar with the text of a nonaggression pact between Ramses II of Egypt and an unknown king named Hattusili III. Ramses had ordered the treaty engraved in hieroglyphs on the walls of the temple at Karnak, and Winckler knew its terms and phrases virtually by memory. He now found himself holding a tablet "in the most beautiful cuneiform script and in good Babylonian!" from which those same terms and phrases leaped out at him.

There, matching the Karnak hieroglyphic version almost word for word, were the same lists of Ramses' and Hattusili's titles and ancestors. There, paragraph for paragraph and clause for clause, were the treaty's conditions and agreements. A fragment of a second copy of the treaty also was discovered, and Winckler immediately comprehended why: like all important legal records down to the present day, it would have been filed in duplicate.

Winckler said the event was as wonderful as a fairy story from the *1001 Nights*—and there were more wonders to come. In 1907 he returned to Bogazköy with another expedition. Experience seems not to have improved his excavating method. The actual digging was left to Turkish workmen, who were less than forthright about exactly where the treasures were turning up—and considerably less than painstaking in the handling of them. A European on the team said he followed one of these workers to a section of the dig where he was amazed to see orderly rows of perfectly preserved tablets. The Turk nonchalantly smashed a number of them with his pickax, loaded the pieces into a basket and carried them off to be presented to Winckler.

But even the most slipshod workmanship could not devalue the hoard, so rich was it. In all, more than 10,000 tablets and fragments were retrieved. Again and again the documents surprised Winckler with the names of foreign kings and places and descriptions of events that he was able to identify from Egyptian, Babylonian and Assyrian sources. Wright and Sayce may have guessed wrong about the location of the seat of Hittite power, but here was overwhelming proof of their basic contention—that this nation had been a force to be reckoned with in the ancient world.

From the tablets he could translate with relative ease—those in Akkadian—Winckler also gleaned the names and the deeds of a few Hittite kings, enough to produce an incomplete "king list," the starting point for a reconstruction of Hittite history. But the many documents written in the Arzawa language, which thereafter would be called Hittite, steadfastly held their secrets.

In the little more than 30 years that had elapsed since the finding of the Hamath stones, what had once been measured as only a minor Biblical tribe was now promoted to the first-rank status of a powerful ancient empire. And yet it was still an empire about which very little was known. Not until Arzawan could be read—and the hieroglyphic inscriptions in Hamathite deciphered—would the Hittites emerge from beneath the dust of time.

Amid the Rocks, a Home for the Gods

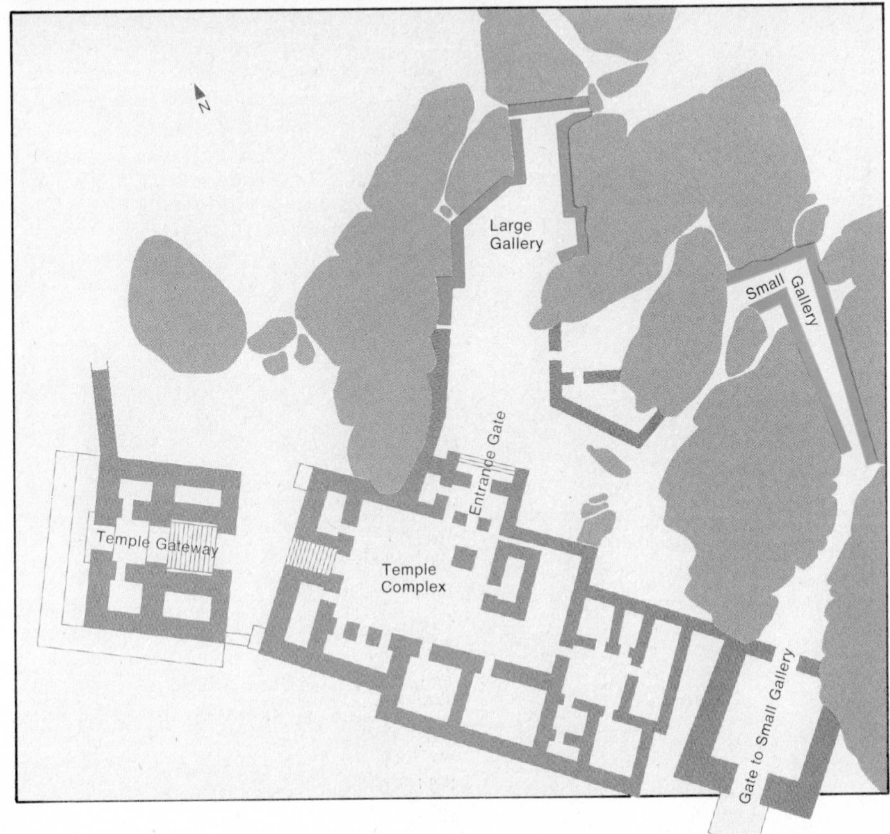

To its discoverer, the 19th Century French explorer Charles-Félix-Marie Texier, Yazilikaya ("inscribed rock" in Turkish) at first appeared to be nothing more than another of the limestone outcroppings in the region around the Hittite capital of Hattusa. But when he ventured beyond the foundations *(foreground, photograph at left)* that mark the site of a temple, he was amazed to find two natural chambers, or galleries, in the rock formation. On the walls of the larger one were carved the figures of 66 gods and goddesses. Texier never did learn that he had come upon the official religious sanctuary of the Hittite kings. Indeed, he thought that the reliefs on those rock walls represented a meeting of Amazons and Paphlagonians, ancient residents of Asia Minor.

The precise arrangement of the shrine is reconstructed in the ground plan *(left, below)*. By placing the temple structures in front of the natural outcropping, the Hittite architects shielded the entrances to the two galleries and helped keep private the rituals that were performed inside.

Temple ruins sprawl outside the entrance to the large gallery (photograph, top). In Hittite days worshipers entered the temple through a main gateway (ground plan, left) and then passed through it to another gate that led into the large gallery. An adjoining small gallery could be reached through narrow passageways or directly, by a separate gate (lower right).

A who's who of Hittite deities, this portion of a Texier engraving includes (from left to right) the Sun God, the Moon God, two handmaidens of the Goddess of War, the Goddess herself and the God of Water. On his cap the Sun God wears a sun disk, symbol of kingship. The hieroglyphs in his left hand mean the Sun God of Heaven.

A Parade of Stone Deities

Stunned by his discovery, Texier made drawings of the reliefs he found in the rock chambers, and they were subsequently published in France as engravings. Although the engraver apparently chose to complete —often incorrectly—certain details that were missing from the weathered and damaged rock originals, the reproductions still constitute a vivid and useful guide to the actual reliefs.

Yazilikaya's most dramatic scenes are found in the awesome setting of the large gallery. Here imaginative Hittite sculptors took advantage of the flanking walls to divide the 66 deities into two stately processions. The division is almost exclusively by sex; gods—some of them marching in lock step and carrying curved slashing swords and most wearing pointed crowns—parade across the length of one wall, goddesses in flowing gowns, across that of the other wall.

Worn by more than 3,000 years of exposure to wind, snow and rain, the carvings in the foreground of the photograph at right were the basis for Texier's engraved reconstruction above. Around the corner of the rock wall, in the background, can be seen another segment of the relief.

Protocol of Divine Status

In addition to separating the deities in the large gallery by sex, the sculptors carefully organized the two processions according to the strict dictates of divine protocol. The males are led by mighty Teshub, the Storm God, and the females by Hebat, the Sun Goddess; the divinities that follow behind each are ranked in hierarchical order, with those of lesser status bringing up the rear.

Where the two columns converge, on a narrow section of wall at the back of the gallery *(below)*, the sculptors treated the scene with all the pomp and respect befitting the meeting between the Hittites' chief deities *(right)*. Both the Storm God and the Sun Goddess hold the insignia of their high offices, including the Hittite hieroglyphs for their names, and even Teshub's two sacred bulls, standing between them, wear the pointed crowns of male gods.

Struck by the sunshine that reaches into the large gallery only a few hours each day, this damaged relief—in which the male and female deities meet—is the rock shrine's principal scene.

Exuding power, Teshub, the Storm God (second figure from left), stands on a pair of bowed mountain gods, while Hebat, his consort, has her feet planted firmly on the back of a panther. Trailing Teshub is the Storm God of Hattusa perched on two flat-topped mountains; to the right of Hebat are her son, also riding a panther, and her two daughters, who seem to float above the double-headed eagle, a possible symbol of Hittite royalty.

An engraving shows but part of the sword relief (right).

The Place of the Dead

Yazilikaya's small gallery, which served as a shrine to the dead, may once have held the remains of King Tudhaliya. His image is carved there in the fatherly embrace of an oversized god *(far right)*. The chamber's mortuary purpose may also account for a curious carving on another of the walls—a sword *(near right)*, whose blade seemingly disappears into the rock itself. The arrangement suggests a reference to the underworld; the Sword God seems to have been one of the Hittite deities associated with the infernal region. Hittite priests sought to communicate with such spirits through holes dug in the ground.

The elaborate grip of the carved sword (left) includes twin lions and the profile of a deity who may well be the Sword God. He wears a crown with remnants of four horns on it, signifying lower rank in the Hittite pantheon.

The god Sharruma (right), wearing a crown with six horns running up its front, holds King Tudhaliya to himself with a protective arm and clasps the king's wrist to guide him. The king's father, Hattusili III, ordered the construction of the sanctuary around 1260 B.C.; Tudhaliya saw to its completion some 30 years later.

Chapter Three: Tongues That Would Not Speak

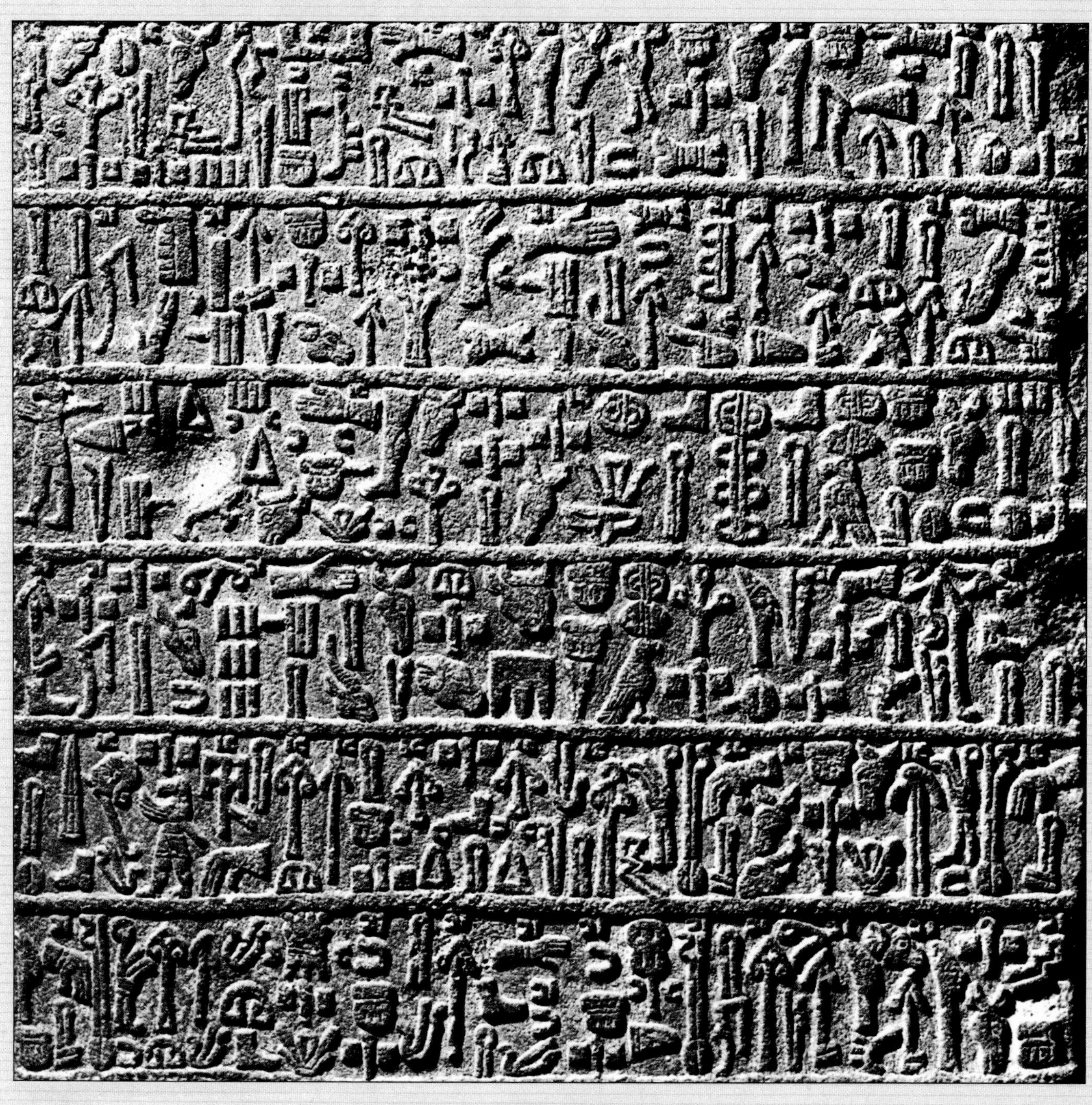

The numerous cuneiform clay tablets in the Arzawa tongue, found by Hugo Winckler in the ruins of Hattusa, were not the only riddles left behind to tease and torment those who tried to divine the secrets of the Hittites. The hieroglyphic inscriptions, like those reproduced on the opposite page, also resisted decipherment; the difficulty of solving the hieroglyphs was even greater than that of the cuneiform writing. The wedge-shaped cuneiform characters were at least in recognizable script, borrowed by the Hittites from the Babylonians; nobody could even guess at the language used in the hieroglyphs. Yet there the hieroglyphs were—on temple walls and monuments—tantalizing scholars with the possibility that they might convey critical information relating to religion and great historical events.

Attempts to decipher the strange signs had begun as soon as they turned up on the Hamath stones, and there were in fact a few early successes.

In 1874, an American student of ancient languages, William Hayes Ward, discerned the order in which the so-called Hamathite inscriptions were to be read. This advance involved more ingenuity than may at first be apparent. Present-day Western languages are written horizontally and read from left to right. However, when a scholar is confronted by an ancient and unknown language, in an unknown script from an unknown culture, why should he conclude that it was not intended to be read from right to left as are Hebrew and Arabic, or in vertical columns from top to bottom as in Chinese, or even bottom to top?

The Hittite signs and pictures carved on this section of a stone tablet from the city of Carchemish underscore the problems scholars faced when they first attempted to translate Hittite hieroglyphs. Even the order in which the text was to be read confounded them until one man realized that the lines read alternately right to left and then left to right. The clue lay in the reversal of individual signs, such as the outstretched hands in the first, second, third and fourth rows.

Ward noticed that those Hittite hieroglyphs that had recognizable pictorial value—i.e., heads, feet, hands, animals—faced one way on one line and in the opposite direction on the following line. He therefore concluded—and correctly—that the hieroglyphs were to be read *boustrophedon,* "as the ox plows," from right to left along one line and returning along the next line from left to right.

In another early success, in 1876, one of the hieroglyphs on the Hamath stones was deciphered by the British philologist Archibald Henry Sayce. Studying copies of Hamathite inscriptions, he deduced rightly that the symbol, a profile of a man, signified the first person singular pronoun. Thus, after 30 centuries of silence, the Hittites spoke their first word to the modern era: "I."

Regrettably, Sayce later changed his mind about that sign, deciding instead that it meant "I speak." But by 1880, after examining other inscriptions resembling those of the Hamath stones, Sayce was again on the right track. Convinced now that the carvers of the Hamathite hieroglyphs were indeed Hittites, he was able to state with certainty that he had deciphered another symbol: . This, he said, was "the determinative prefix of divinity." In other words, it meant "god." The basis for his conclusion was that the symbol accompanied the godlike images on the rock carvings at Yazilikaya, the Hittite shrine.

Sayce knew that this symbol could be a valuable key for unlocking the meaning of more of the enigmatic signs. He already had figured out that the

Hittites' hieroglyphic system was largely syllabic, that is, most of its symbols stood for single phonetic syllables. There were too many different signs for the system to be based on a simple alphabet, he reasoned, and far too few for it to be altogether ideographic, like Chinese, in which each symbol represents a different word. The same "god" sign had cropped up on the Hamath stones and elsewhere, and always as a prefix to unreadable groups of hieroglyphs that appeared to be the names of deities. Thus, Sayce concluded, if the name of one of these divinities could be ascertained from another language, in which, hopefully, the pronunciation would be similar, then perhaps the rendering of that name in Hittite hieroglyphs could be broken down into its sign-for-syllable components. And the resultant keys in turn could be applied to other parts of a Hittite inscription where the same signs appeared.

Now Sayce yearned for what students of ancient languages call a bilingual, an inscription bearing the same text in two languages, a known one, and one needing interpretation. The most famous bilingual of all time is the Rosetta stone, which was discovered in Egypt in 1799 and which led to the decipherment of Egyptian hieroglyphs (actually it was a trilingual, carrying its message not only in Egyptian hieroglyphs but also in an Egyptian script known as demotic and in readable Greek). It is easy, then, to imagine how excited Sayce was when, in 1880, he found himself on the track of what he hoped would be "the Rosetta stone of Hittite decipherment."

He recalled that eight years earlier, before he even knew that Hittite hieroglyphs existed, he had read a report describing an ancient silver disk that had come to light in Istanbul. According to the report, the relic was small and looked as if it might have been used as a seal *(page 55)*. In its center was the figure of a warrior and around its rim ran a cuneiform inscription in a readable dialect of Hurrian. Sayce dug out the old report and read it again.

The second reading disclosed details that formerly had conveyed no special meaning to him: according to the description, the warrior on the seal wore a short tunic, a cloak, a helmet—and boots with turned-up toes. Sayce now recognized the dress as Hittite.

But what sent his imagination and his hopes soaring was the author's account of the signs on the seal: "goats' heads . . . a palm-branch . . . four vertical lines and one horizontal line, which I conjecture must represent grains of wheat; next between the shoulder and the spear, we have a sort of obelisk."

Hittite hieroglyphs! Sayce was certain. He had seen those symbols before, in copies of the inscriptions found at Carchemish, Hamath and Aleppo, and in 1879 he himself had scrambled up the cliff near Smyrna in western Turkey *(page 32)* to take firsthand impressions of similar symbols. If, as Sayce suspected, the cuneiform on the seal and the Hittite characters also on it conveyed the same meaning, he had what he longed for: a bilingual.

He had one, that is, if he could find the silver seal —or the next best thing, an accurate copy of it. With the determination of a Scotland Yard man on the trail of an archcriminal, the philologist started his legwork. The report, itself eight years old in 1880, referred to another, prior account that included a drawing of the seal.

After several days' search Sayce finally located the earlier report. One look at the drawing clearly bore out his supposition that the symbols on the seal were

Boldly inscribed with both Hittite hieroglyphs and wedge-shaped cuneiform characters, this small silver seal mounted on a clay base provided the first key to the puzzle of the Hittite language. The cuneiform around the rim, which could be deciphered, led to the translation of the hieroglyphs in the inner circle. Both read: "Tarriktimme, king of the country of Erme."

Hittite hieroglyphs, but Sayce was unwilling to trust the accuracy of the artist's effort at copying the seal's cuneiform. Through a scholarly British publication he appealed for help: Did anyone know the whereabouts of the seal itself? No, one reader replied, but he knew the British Museum had been offered it 20 years before and had turned it down, thinking it might be a fake. A man at the museum, however, had made a facsimile of it.

The copy still existed, but the circumstances surrounding its making were hazy, and now Sayce feared it might have been reproduced from a poorly made plaster cast instead of from the genuine article. His anxiety was dispelled when a Frenchman who had seen the original seal in Istanbul sent Sayce an excellent plaster cast he himself had made of it. This cast agreed completely with the facsimile.

Once satisfied with the accuracy of the copies, Sayce translated the cuneiform as "Tarriktimme, king of the country of Erme." (Nowadays scholars read the name as Tarkumuwa, and the seal—the original turned up in the 1920s and is now in a Baltimore museum—is known as the Tarkumuwa seal.)

Having translated the cuneiform inscription, Sayce turned to the hieroglyphs on each side of the seal's warrior-king and soon was able to confirm a suspicion aroused by other Hittite hieroglyphs: that a triangle with a cross in it meant "king," and that two triangles marked with stripes meant "country," or "land." The latter eventually led him to guess that another symbol, a single striped triangle he had seen elsewhere, meant "city." In time he was proved correct on all counts.

Unfortunately, that was about the full extent of the Tarkumuwa seal's contribution, and it was not enough to solve the mystery of hieroglyphic Hittite. Although the seal was something of a disappointment as a bilingual, and although many of Sayce's subsequent efforts were to be criticized by scholars, his achievement nevertheless was remarkable. By the end of 1880 he had correctly interpreted six hieroglyphic characters in a totally unknown system of writing (seven, including his original reading of "I"): besides the four nouns, he had isolated the symbols denoting accusative and nominative word endings.

The measure of his accomplishment can be gauged from the length of time it took a worldful of scholars to progress significantly beyond that point. "It cannot be long before the inscriptions left to us by the Hittites, in their peculiar form of hieroglyphic writing, are . . . made to reveal their secrets," Sayce said in 1888. But even though he lived to be an old man, at the time of his death in 1933 the stubborn script had yielded only a few more bits of meaning. In fact, not until three decades later—almost a hundred years after the symbols came to the world's attention—could anyone state convincingly that the decipherment of Hittite hieroglyphs was well in hand.

Thanks partly to Winckler's discovery of the cuneiform archives at Hattusa (the Hittite capital at Bogazköy) and partly to an obscure Austrian army lieutenant's regard for scholarship, the world did not have to depend upon the decipherment of the hieroglyphs for information about the Hittites.

Hugo Winckler, as a philologist and as the finder of the cuneiform tablets, naturally had wanted first crack at deciphering the so-called Arzawa tongue. But bad health severely curtailed his work and, jealous of competitors, he was apparently reluctant to

Solving the Key Puzzle of Hittite Cuneiform

Deciphering Hittite cuneiform was a problem almost as difficult as interpreting the hieroglyphs. Although the characters were the same as those in readable Babylonian, the words were untranslatable; no one had an inkling of their meaning. The major obstacle was the lack of a key, such as a detailed bilingual: an inscription in two languages, one of which could be read. Without such an aid, scholars had to pore over tablets looking for clues. A breakthrough came in 1915 when a Czech researcher—after painstaking study—announced that Hittite was an Indo-European language, related to other known tongues. Slowly thereafter Hittite surrendered its vocabulary and grammar, and by the 1930s, when several bilinguals were studied in detail *(opposite)*, scholars could at last read it with some facility.

Found in Egypt around 1890, this tablet was one of two that brought the Hittite tongue to the attention of scholars. It deals with a marriage proposal between a pharaoh and a princess of Arzawa, a sometime vassal state of the Hittites.

THE WISE WORDS OF KING HATTUSILI I

About 1640 B.C. the great Hittite ruler Hattusili I dismissed his nephew, the heir apparent, and named his grandson Mursili I as successor. The following excerpts are drawn from Hattusili's lengthy political testament, one of the most eloquent Hittite documents yet discovered. He speaks to both Mursili and the senate:

"You must keep my words! As long as you keep them, Hattusa will stand tall, and you will make your land be at peace. . . . If you do not keep them, your land will pass under foreign control. Give careful attention to the words of the gods! Their sacrificial loaves, their libations, their cakes, and their flour must always be set up. . . . Let them read this tablet aloud in your presence month by month. . . . My son, what is in your heart, do always."

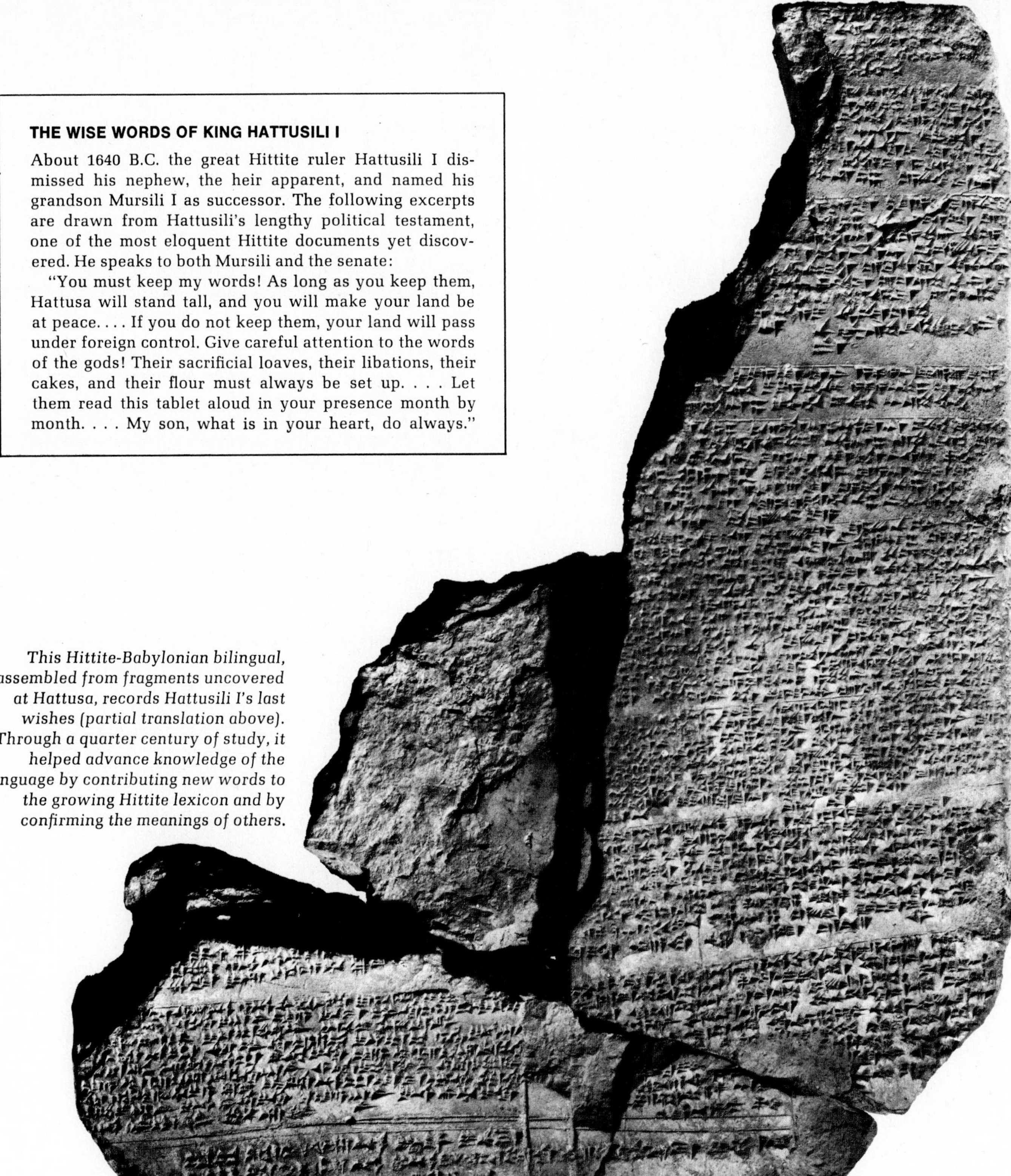

This Hittite-Babylonian bilingual, assembled from fragments uncovered at Hattusa, records Hattusili I's last wishes (partial translation above). Through a quarter century of study, it helped advance knowledge of the language by contributing new words to the growing Hittite lexicon and by confirming the meanings of others.

turn over the task to others. When Winckler died in 1913, no notes or manuscripts on the clay documents could be found among his papers.

The German Oriental Society, which had sponsored his expeditions to the Hittite capital, then called in a number of Assyriologists to work on the tablets. One of them was a 35-year-old, Polish-born Czech named Bedrich Hrozny. The son of a cleric, Hrozny had begun his academic career studying theology, as his father wished. Soon, however, his passion for courses in Hebrew and Arabic led him into ancient Oriental languages, and at the age of 24 he became a professor of Assyriology at the University of Vienna. But what especially fascinated Hrozny was the problem of Hittite cuneiform. Thus in 1914 he was delighted to be sent to Istanbul, where most of the Bogazköy tablets in the Arzawa language were stored, to aid in the work of decipherment. Addressing himself directly to the problem, Hrozny chose to attack the mystery not by using the tablets in Babylonian, which could be read, but by working on those in the Hittites' own lost tongue. Fortunately, a few Babylonian words had been incorporated into the Arzawa language and one of these words provided Hrozny with a critical key. It appeared in a sentence that was to become one of the most famous in the history of philology. The word was *ninda*—"bread." The sentence that contained it—written, it should be remembered, in cuneiform characters that could be pronounced, if not understood—was *nu ninda-an ezzateni watar-ma ekuteni.*

Before he analyzed this passage Hrozny had already begun to develop some ideas about the unknown language with which he was struggling, thoughts so unorthodox that he had suppressed them. Similar thoughts had indeed been voiced in 1902 by a Norwegian, J. A. Knudtzon, who had studied the Arzawa tablets found in Egypt among the Tell el-Amarna letters. But Knudtzon had folded under the pressure of academic criticism and recanted.

Instrumental in shaping Hrozny's ideas was his firm grasp of linguistic science in general, an understanding that embraced not only the Semitic languages with which he had dealt as an Assyriologist but the Indo-European languages as well. Familiar with the interrelationships within that linguistic family, he knew how similarities in vocabulary and grammatical forms proved that tongues as seemingly unconnected as Icelandic and Sanskrit had evolved from the same source.

Now as Hrozny read and reread the Hittite sentence—*nu ninda-an ezzateni watar-ma ekuteni*—a growing suspicion that he was looking at an Indo-European language crystallized into near-certainty. The evidence before him seemed so striking that he allowed his daring to overcome his caution.

The suffix *-an*, for example, in several other contexts had seemed to denote the accusative case (as did *-n* in Greek, an Indo-European language). Since *ninda*, the word for "bread," was an object, then something was being done to it. What do you usually do to bread? You eat it.

Fishing in his mind for Indo-European words meaning "eat," Hrozny reviewed the catch: English *eat*, Greek *edein*, Latin *edere*, medieval German—*ezzan*. *Ezzanteni!* He had already decided that *teni* was a verb ending, which fit perfectly. It was a heady moment, but as a scholar Hrozny could not let a similarity that might be no more than coincidence deflect him from continued objective examination.

Flanked by stones that bear Hittite inscriptions, figures of a seated dignitary and attendant and those of two warriors guard fortress ruins atop Black Mountain in southern Turkey. It was here that the decisive key to Hittite hieroglyphs turned up—messages both in Hittite symbols and in the readable script of the Phoenicians.

Although Americans arrived late on the scene of Hittite studies, they made an immediate contribution of their own—the automobile. In the 1926 snapshot at right archeologists set out to explore Hittite sites in a loaded vehicle—only to run into trouble (opposite). But despite such setbacks, they did excavate a site, and they could say that thanks to the modern auto they had been able to penetrate regions not before visited by archeologists.

The passage appeared to be rhetorically balanced. It even rhymed. From previously considered sentences he had picked out the word *nu* and the suffix *-ma* as having some kind of relationship, like the relationship of "here" and "there," or "now" and "then."

That would make sense in a two-part message. "Now bread . . . eat . . . then." After getting that far, no amount of devotion to scientific discipline could have restrained Hrozny's intuition. There was no need to ask himself what goes with "bread" or to list mentally the terms for it in Indo-European tongues. The word was there, staring him in the face: Hittite *watar*, German *wasser*, English *water*. It tumbled into place.

"Now bread you eat; water then you drink."

Although Hrozny had not yet deciphered Arzawan, he had reached a conclusion so astounding that the repercussions in the philological establishment were sure to be earsplitting. But at this point World War I threatened to impose a long and disagreeable interruption on his work; European governments had better things for their young men to do than pore over old clay tablets in dusty museums. So on November 24, 1915, Hrozny announced his findings. At a meeting in Berlin of the Near Eastern Society he declared that Hittite was an Indo-European language. The reaction, as he had expected, was mainly one of outrage. He was attacked for his presumption; if Hittite were an Indo-European language, it would be the oldest Indo-European language ever discovered (at that time it was, since its only challengers, the related Luwian and Palaic dialects, were then unknown). He was also ignoring racial evidence, his colleagues insisted; the Hittites as depicted in their rock carvings were obviously of Armenian stock (they were not). The debate lasted far into the night. At its end, Hrozny had not convinced his critics.

Seven days later he was drafted into the Austro-Hungarian army. Had he spent the war pushing artillery through the blood-soaked mud of Europe, years would have passed before he could substantiate his claims—if, indeed, he lived to substantiate them at all. But at this juncture Hrozny—and Hittitology—came into an incredible bit of good fortune.

Because he had poor eyesight, Hrozny was made a clerk in the Vienna garrison regiment. His superior, one Lieutenant Kammergruber, displaying a tolerance for intellectuals uncharacteristic of the military, relieved him of most of his duties and told him to get on with his scholarship. Later Hrozny publicly acknowledged his gratitude for Kammergruber's "understanding consideration"—and well he might have.

Because of the lieutenant's indulgence, Hrozny was able to publish his preliminary report before the end of 1915, and in 1917, while the war still raged across Europe, to bring out a book called *The Language of the Hittites: Its Structure and Its Membership in the Indo-European Linguistic Family*. Rarely had a dead language been treated so comprehensively. Hrozny not only roughly defined the position of the Hittites within the Indo-European language group, but detailed the grammatical structure of their tongue.

His detractors, however, were not yet stilled. They continued to assail his radical thesis, and some of their criticism was valid. Hrozny, not being a specialist in Indo-European languages, fell into errors of detail that damaged his credibility. But far from being intimidated by the storm he had stirred up, Hrozny proceeded to translate the Bogazköy tablets. In 1919 he published his first lengthy translations of Hittite cuneiform texts and won his first converts. The next year Ferdinand Sommer, a distinguished German Indo-Europeanist, came over to Hrozny's side, providing the expertise in Indo-European languages that Hrozny lacked and correcting many of his particulars. From then on Hrozny's case gained more and more advocates; today it has no serious opposition. And the documents translated by him and others at last provided the first glimpses into the history of the Hittites.

While the clay tablets from Bogazköy finally were being compelled to speak, the Hittite hieroglyphs remained as intransigently silent as ever, and not because they escaped study.

By collecting and editing all the known inscriptions, a German antiquarian named Leopold Messerschmidt in 1900 performed a major service: he published all of them in a single volume. Before the appearance of his *Corpus Inscriptionum Hettiticarum,* would-be decipherers—unless they had time, money and the inclination to visit widely scattered sites and museums—had to make do with limited materials. Thanks to Messerschmidt the new availability of the texts enabled philologists from all over the world to join the offensive on hieroglyphic Hittite. Even with this renewed pressure, however, the rewards were squeezed out only in isolated driblets—a place name or two, recognition of some Hittite punctuation marks, but nothing to harbinger victory.

This near-stalemate finally was broken in the early 1930s as a new generation of scholars, representing many nationalities, saw the hieroglyphs as an opportunity for original achievement. None of these men singlehandedly deciphered the hieroglyphs, but the cumulative result of their studies showed more progress toward a solution in a few years than had been made in the prior half century.

For example, Piero Meriggi, an Italian, isolated the signs that meant "son" and "grandson," a discovery that helped lead to the decipherment of several royal names. And an ingenious Swiss scholar, Emil Forrer, discovered striking parallels between some Babylonian cuneiform writings and Hittite hieroglyphs. Forrer knew that different ancient peoples used the same or very similar formulas for phrasing standard items, like curses or the introductions to letters. The Babylonian king Hammurabi, for instance, at the close of a famous inscription of his laws, stated that if anyone should erase or ignore them "be he a king, be he a lord . . . may Anu, the powerful father of the gods, take from him the title of king, break his sceptre and curse his fate."

Studying Hittite hieroglyphic inscriptions, Forrer

During a break from their digging on Karatepe, German and Turkish archeologists stand with their leader, Helmuth Bossert (holding glasses), discoverer of the site. Only after they had collected numerous inscriptions in Hittite hieroglyphs and translatable Phoenician writing did philologist Franz Steinherr (far right) realize—during a dream —that a pair of texts in the two languages were identical, thus providing the key to the hitherto unfathomable Hittite.

came across a clause that he believed meant "be he a king or a prince," followed by groups of signs that included the plural of the determinative for "god." Deducing that it was a curse along the same lines as Hammurabi's, Forrer was able to peel the inscription down to its skeletal form and pick out the symbols representing different verb endings. Applying this kind of dissection-by-comparison to several pieces of text, he managed to uncover the grammatical structure of the language recorded by the hieroglyphs.

The validity of the work being done by Meriggi, Forrer and others was graphically revealed when several of them worked independently on the same texts. For the first time since the assault on the hieroglyphs had begun, decipherers were coming up with readings that agreed. At last, in a very real sense they were all speaking the same language.

That it was the right language was dramatically confirmed in 1934 when Kurt Bittel, a German archeologist, resumed Winckler's work in the ruins of Hattusa. In the remains of the royal palace he found about 300 clay seals. The news that 100 of them were genuine bilinguals electrified Hittitologists. Most of the inscriptions were too short to supply many new interpretations, but by providing the names of kings in both hieroglyphic and cuneiform versions, they demonstrated beyond doubt that the decipherers had been reading the royal names correctly, that the system they were evolving was the right one.

At the end of World War II, the conquest of hieroglyphic Hittite was far from complete. A specialist in ancient languages still could not pick up a copy of one of the texts and translate it completely. However, a firm beachhead had been established. The basic grammatical system was understood, and many groups of the hieroglyphic symbols could be read.

It had taken 70 years to achieve this much, and all of it the hard way—without the aid of a bilingual of any decent length. But at this point luck at long last decided to smile on those who would unlock the full message of the hieroglyphs.

In the summer of 1945 a small exploring party from the University of Istanbul, led by Helmuth Bossert, a German-born professor, was roaming through the Taurus Mountains of southern Turkey. Bossert's mission was something of a fishing expedition; he was seeking signs of Hittite civilization in a little-visited region. Just as the French explorer Texier had done more than a century before, Bossert questioned local inhabitants for possible leads to ancient remains. At a small village called Feke some nomads told him of a "lion stone" that stood on a wooded mountain near the town of Kadirli.

This information set his historian's antennae aquiver. The lion, he knew, was a frequent subject of Hittite sculpture. Frustrated to learn that summer rains made the road to Kadirli impassable, Bossert resolved to return as soon as possible. When he and his party came back the following February, the local people told him that recent rains had again made the road a quagmire. Bossert insisted he could not wait and set off in a horse-drawn wagon. The wagon sank to its axles in mud; the driver became hopelessly lost and the horses collapsed. Bossert's group found another driver and team, and pushed on. Again they bogged down, but by walking much of the distance and by occasionally pushing the wagon, they reached Kadirli by nightfall—only to be told that no one there had ever heard of a lion stone or of any other old relics in the vicinity.

Exhausted and disappointed, Bossert was almost ready to accept defeat when he met a local schoolteacher whose wanderings had made him unusually familiar with the region. Yes, the schoolteacher said, he knew of the lion stone. He had seen it himself no less than four times. It was a six-hour ride away on a peak called Karatepe—Black Mountain—and he would lead them there the next day *(page 59)*.

He did, and at the top of the forest-darkened peak Bossert saw not only the "lion stone"—it turned out to be a bull—but also the badly damaged human figure that once had surmounted it. And on this broken statue he found an inscription. Bossert recognized the writing as a Semitic script scholars could read, but he himself did not know the language (later he would learn it was Phoenician). And yet the style of the sculpture was distinctly Hittite. Searching the area, he and his companions found other fragments of worked stone—but now inscribed with hieroglyphs. The possible significance of this discovery—the juxtaposition of a known script and hieroglyphic Hittite—stirred the group with excitement. But they were in the wilderness without equipment, and night was approaching. Bossert decided to leave and return with an outfitted party, to dig at Black Mountain.

He came back in 1947 and soon found fortification walls, the walls of buildings, large reliefs of human and animal figures, and part of another Phoenician inscription. Later that year, near the buried gate of what apparently had been a Hittite fortress, the excavators uncovered the rest of the second Phoenician inscription—which proved to be the longest-running text in that language ever found. And near it were other lengthy texts—in hieroglyphic Hittite.

The anticipation that these closely associated finds might provide the long-sought bilingual was not to be quickly satisfied. Unable to read Phoenician, Bossert sent copies of the text to experts who could. Even when he had received their translations, he could not say for sure that he had found a bilingual. The Phoenician words were those of a local neo-Hittite ruler named Asitiwatta, who boasted that he had "wiped out all the evil that was in the land" and had provided "plenty and goodness and good living and ease of heart" for his people. The same name, Asitiwatta, could be deciphered in the hieroglyphic version, but beyond that there seemed to be nothing to indicate that the texts were alike.

The link that intimately connected the texts was discovered not by a professional philologist but by an amateur (admittedly, a well-educated one) who said that he found it, literally, in his sleep.

Franz Steinherr was the bookkeeper at the German hospital in Istanbul when Bossert accepted him as a volunteer at the Black Mountain dig. For months Steinherr studied the texts found there until entire passages from both the Phoenician script and the hieroglyphs were engraved in his memory.

One day Steinherr attended a lecture during which Bossert discussed a phrase from a Phoenician inscription: "and I made horse go with horse, and shield with shield, and army with army." That night before going to bed, Steinherr studied Hittite hieroglyphic texts for hours. After sleeping for a while, he suddenly found himself wide awake with a clear image of some of the pictorial symbols in his mind—two horses' heads and the signs for "I made." The latter were among the few symbols that Hittitologists had already learned to read, but no one else working at Black Mountain had yet recognized them among the inscriptions already found.

"I made horse go with horse." Here was the key, the very combination of words that Bossert had been expounding from the Phoenician version the previous afternoon, expressed in Hittite hieroglyphs. Black Mountain had produced a bilingual.

This bolt of lightning did not immediately illuminate all the dark corners of hieroglyphic Hittite. But the Black Mountain discovery so enlarged the known vocabulary of the hieroglyphic script and so increased the understanding of its syntax that by the 1960s scholars could say with certainty that the mystery was solved. The strange symbols that had puzzled Texier at Bogazköy, intrigued Wright at Hamath, fascinated Sayce and perplexed other scholars for almost a century now could be interpreted. The messages carved on stone obviously had been intended for posterity, and posterity—probably a far more distant one than Hittite scribes ever imagined—could read them at last.

The Majestic Reaches of the Hittites' Far-flung Lands

A steep river valley carpeted with poplars cuts the Anatolian plateau near the site of Kanesh, a trading center in early Hittite days.

When the Hittite monarch toured his empire, he saw landscapes almost as diverse as the peoples he ruled. At the zenith of its power, around the 14th Century B.C., that empire covered an area as large as present-day France and England, and stretched from the shores of the Black Sea deep into Syria and from the Aegean as far as the upper reaches of the Euphrates River. It embraced more than a dozen conquered or subservient kingdoms, with such strange-sounding names as Pitassa and Kizzuwatna.

Within the imperial boundaries lay vast expanses of rolling, grassy plains, towering mountain peaks perennially capped with snow and deeply gashed with cliff-bound valleys, barren desert lands and stretches of rugged coast. In the region known today as Cappadocia, to the south of the Hittites' capital of Hattusa, the scenery was moonlike: here erosion had carved the soft volcanic rock into shapes that suggest cones, pyramids, or the petrified waves of a choppy sea.

Tortured formations of volcanic tuff, sculpted by wind and weather, rise out of the floor of the Göreme Valley in Cappadocia, a bizarre area that lay at the heart of the Hittite homeland. In the 19th and 18th centuries B.C. Assyrian merchant colonies, known as karums, flourished in the region.

The fertile plain and terraced hillsides near modern Antakya (the Antioch of antiquity) in northwestern Syria once were ruled by princes allied to Mitanni, a long-time enemy of the Hittites. This rich land finally fell to armies led by one of the greatest of the Hittite empire builders, Suppiluliuma I.

Its scarred, rocky flanks blanketed by snow, the peak of Hasan Dagi looms above the Anatolian plateau north of the Taurus Mountains. Known to the Hittites as the Lower Land, this area still supports large herds of sheep, once a mainstay of the Hittite economy.

The 17th Century Hittite warrior-king Labarna I "subdued the lands of his enemies with might . . . and made the seas his frontiers." In the process this rocky stretch of Mediterranean coast in south-central Turkey, near the small modern port of Alanya (seen at upper left), probably fell under his sway.

Against a background of hills streaked with cultivated fields, oxcarts with solid wooden wheels—similar to those used by the Hittites—creak across a mountain-ringed plain near Erzurum in northeastern Turkey. Conquered by Suppiluliuma I, this region formed a vassal kingdom of the Hittite Empire.

Chapter Four: The Art of Empire Building

As more and more of the clay tablets and hieroglyphic inscriptions gave up their long-held secrets, an overwhelming truth came clear: the Hittites had been empire builders of the first magnitude. Their homeland was rich in both minerals and agricultural products, but their ambition for still greater wealth and for power drove them to expand their borders far beyond the land of Hatti.

At its peak, around 1300 B.C., Hittite hegemony encompassed an area almost the size of modern France and England together. This was an astonishingly great amount of territory to bring under one rule, considering the primitive communications of the period, but the Hittites managed—in large measure because of the unusually civilized way their rulers went about the business of empire building.

Ironic as it may seem to attribute restraint to warriors who sacked Babylon, who dominated Anatolia and Syria and who ultimately stood off Egypt's legions, the fact is that the Hittites were as skilled with words as they were with weapons. Their contemporaries recognized them as master diplomats—although diplomacy in the ancient world was not always conducted in the genteel manner that it usually is today. At a time when superior power was generally regarded as sufficient excuse for one city-state to take up arms and overrun a neighbor, the Hittites often achieved their ends through negotiations, or perhaps through powerful, nonviolent persuasion. At least three of their neighboring states apparently volunteered for Hittite vassalage. What threats underlay the decision, no one can be sure, because the rulers of Hatti were certainly not above saber rattling. The willingness of the kingdoms to subjugate themselves may have stemmed from the widespread knowledge that although the Hittites did not indulge in murderous rampages, they did make a practice of burning and looting conquered cities and marching the residents home with them as serfs.

States less eager to submit to Hittite rule first received written challenges, backed up by logical—to the Hittites at least—reasons. The excuse most frequently given for Hittite incursions was that the independent state had transgressed by harboring fugitives from Hittite lands. King Mursili II, one of the Hittites' most effective expansionists, issued such a challenge in 1345 B.C. to the ruler of the neighboring kingdom of Arzawa. In an indignant letter, Mursili declared war: "My subjects who went over to you, when I demanded them back from you, you did not restore them to me; and you called me a child and made light of me. Up then! Let us fight, and let the Storm God, my lord, decide our case."

As it happened, opinion in Arzawa had been divided, half of it inclined to succumb to Hittite dominion, half of it staunchly resistant. Nevertheless, Arzawa did fight. After the dust of battle cleared, the victorious Mursili meted out justice. Those leaders who had given in he left undisturbed, except for conscripting their soldiers. Those who had resisted, he took prisoner. When Mursili recounted the incident years later, he wrote: "The total of civilian captives that I, My Majesty, brought back to the royal palace was altogether 66,000, but what the lords, the sol-

In a scene embossed on the back of a gold-plated throne, Ankhesenamun, queen of Egypt, tenderly ministers to her young husband, King Tutankhamen. When Tutankhamen died, his widow asked to marry a son of the mighty Hittite king Suppiluliuma. The politically beneficial union did not take place, and so the two empires remained rivals.

diers and the charioteers of Hattusa brought back in the way of civilian captives, oxen and sheep—there was no counting it."

Thus Arzawa became another vassal state. Satellite countries, whether they came under Hittite control peaceably or violently, were stitched into the imperial fabric with written words, and Arzawa was no exception. Treaties, rare or even unknown in other parts of the ancient Near East, outlined precisely the nature of the relationship between Hatti and the annexed land. Often when a pact was drawn up its terms were inscribed on tablets of silver, gold or iron (which had not yet become a commonplace, utilitarian material). Clay copies of the document were then filed in the principal temples of both Hattusa and the capital city of the newly acquired state, where they were safeguarded from theft. The loss of a treaty tablet could mean disgrace for a subject king. At least one, the ruler of a north Syrian state, was protected from such ignominy by the explicit terms of the treaty itself: it obliged him to take the document out of storage at regular intervals and read it aloud to an assembly of his princes and courtiers in order to remind them of their commitments to the Hittite ruler.

Although it was the Hittites' customary—and singularly prudent—practice to leave the king of a conquered state, or one of his relatives, in authority over his own people, the content of most treaties left little doubt as to who was in charge. Only when a Hittite king regarded his opponent with respect did the treaty between them reflect a spirit close to fraternal deference. More often, the protocols were calculated to browbeat and humiliate.

The treaties—of which at least 35 have been discovered and translated—followed a standard formula. Most of them introduced the Hittite monarch in immodest language. A typical example is the contract binding the kingdom of Amurru and its king, Duppi-Teshub, to Hatti. The pact begins with these words: "Thus speaks His Majesty, Mursili, Great King, king of the land of Hatti, beloved of the Storm God, son of Suppiluliuma, Great King, King of Hatti, Hero."

There were reasons of course for such hyperbole. The sobriquet "Great King" was no mere expression of self-aggrandizement. Anyone entitled to it was understood by all to be a king over other kings, a monarch who governed a network of kingdoms. The terms "Hero" and "beloved of the Storm God" reflected the fact that the Hittite king saw himself, as did his subjects, to be the specially chosen instrument in peace and in war of the chief deity in the Hittite pantheon. Even the term "His Majesty" was no common form of address. Literally translated, the Hittite word meant that the king acted, with power conferred by the Sun God, as chief judge over Hatti and its dependencies.

In keeping with the formula, King Mursili's treaty with Duppi-Teshub of Amurru includes an extensive review of relations between the two kingdoms over the years, reiterating all the favors and the debts that Amurru owes Hatti. Ultimately, the contract arrives at the terms that are to govern the relationship in the future. Amurru's soldiers shall fight in the Hittite army. Should Hittite soldiers be called upon to defend Amurru, they shall be provided by Duppi-Teshub with food and drink. Should a rash of anti-Hittite sentiment occur in the subject nation, King Duppi-Teshub or one of his brothers must personally quell it, by force if necessary. If a fugitive flees from Hatti to Amurru, he must be extradited. Amurru must

The mark of a mighty man, the seal of Suppiluliuma I, makes official this 14th Century B.C. treaty tablet between the Hittites and the Syrian kingdom of Ugarit. The seal was pressed into the wet clay and the cuneiform characters were added around it. The language is Akkadian, lingua franca of the day.

provide safe passage for any person seeking refuge in the land of Hatti. And so on.

The treaty's next-to-last entry is an admonition: "If Duppi-Teshub does not keep these words of the obligation and of the oath, may these divine oaths destroy Duppi-Teshub . . . his wife, his son, his grandson, his house, his city, his land and everything that belongs to him." After threatening disaster, the treaty ends on a more promising note: "If Duppi-Teshub keeps these words . . . may these divine oaths keep you." And divine they are, for no fewer than 80 gods and goddesses, representing both Hatti and the land of Amurru, are invoked as witnesses to the contract.

As the threat to Duppi-Teshub makes clear, Hittite diplomacy cloaked a belligerent nature—and it was with belligerence as much as with diplomacy that the Hittite Empire was built. Most of the story of its expansion is about warfare.

Military technology in the ancient Near East was well advanced by the 17th Century B.C. when the Hittites emerged as a force to be reckoned with. Hittite generals never hesitated to adopt and adapt the inventions of their predecessors, their allies and their enemies, and so the Hittites became the beneficiaries of more than 1,000 years of other peoples' ingenuity, supplemented with considerable skill of their own.

Hittite troops—under the direction of the king himself—entered battle armed with quivers of bronze-tipped arrows and flexible, high-powered bows made of wood, horn and sinew. For close combat, the infantry carried bronze-bladed daggers, lances, spears, sickle-shaped swords and battle-axes shaped like human hands (*page 77*). Soldiers were protected by bronze armor (metal was in great supply in Anatolia) consisting of a rounded, rectangular shield and a conical helmet with ear flaps and a long, pigtail-like strip that extended down the back of the neck.

The Hittites were masters of siege warfare, and they built battering rams that could breach the fortifying walls of enemy cities. What they could not do with battering rams they accomplished with sheer endurance. Supplied by baggage trains of pack asses and ox-drawn wagons, they could besiege a city for weeks if necessary, until its citizens came out begging for food and water.

The Hittites' crucial military vehicle was the lightweight, single-axle chariot that rolled on two spoked wheels made of wood rimmed with metal—a Mesopotamian invention of about 1800 B.C. The horses that drew these speedy, maneuverable chariots were magnificently trained. One manual used by the Hittites—actually the work of a citizen of the rival Mitannian kingdom—went so far as to detail what the horse trainer should do every waking hour of every day for 90 full days to build up an animal's speed and endurance. It told how fast to run the horse each day and over what distance, how to prepare his feed, when to bridle or unbridle him, when to groom and rub down his coat with oil, when to wash him with water—and when to cover him with a blanket.

Helped by such military sophistication, a king with a deceptively lyrical mouthful of a name, Suppiluliuma, was able in the 14th Century B.C. to raise Hatti to true imperial status. Suppiluliuma's stature as a governor, a general, a diplomat—as well as his foibles as a man—make him stand out as a fully fleshed figure against the all-too-often two-dimensional backdrop of Hittite history.

He was not the first Hittite to try his hand at empire building, nor the first to have success. Suppiluliuma could look back proudly to predecessors who had brought powerful neighboring states to their knees. There was, for example, Labarna I, who extended Hittite hegemony across southern Anatolia to the Mediterranean and westward into the kingdom of Arzawa in the 17th Century B.C. After Labarna I came his son, Labarna II, who marched southeast over the Taurus Mountains to Aleppo, established his capital at Hattusa, and then changed his name to Hattusili. His heir, Mursili I, pushed farther south into Syria. More amazingly, Mursili marched 500 miles down the Euphrates River, razed Babylon, Mesopotamia's most awesome city, and then, for reasons not clearly understood, turned tail, without ever establishing suzerainty over Babylon's smoldering ruins.

After this short succession of triumphant leaders, the Hittite kingdom lapsed into 200 years of almost uninterrupted disorder. King Mursili I was assassinated by his brother-in-law, who seized the throne. In the latter's wake followed a sequence of impotent kings. As they struggled to save the crown from ambitious princes and nobles, Hatti's international prestige dwindled and many of its conquests reverted to domestic or foreign rule.

All the while, the kingdom of Mitanni, some 300 miles to the southeast in northern Syria, had been launching corrosive little raids on the fringes of Hittite territory and gradually beating the Hittites back into their Anatolian homeland. Eventually an alliance between the Egyptians and the Mitannians placed an outpost of the imperial giant of the Nile right at the Hittites' back door. It was a significant event for Hatti. The time was not far off when the Hittites would

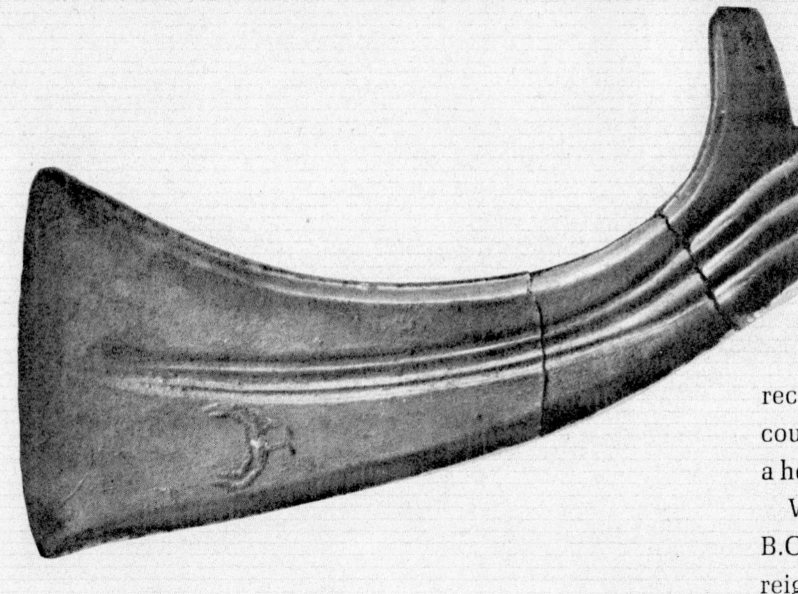

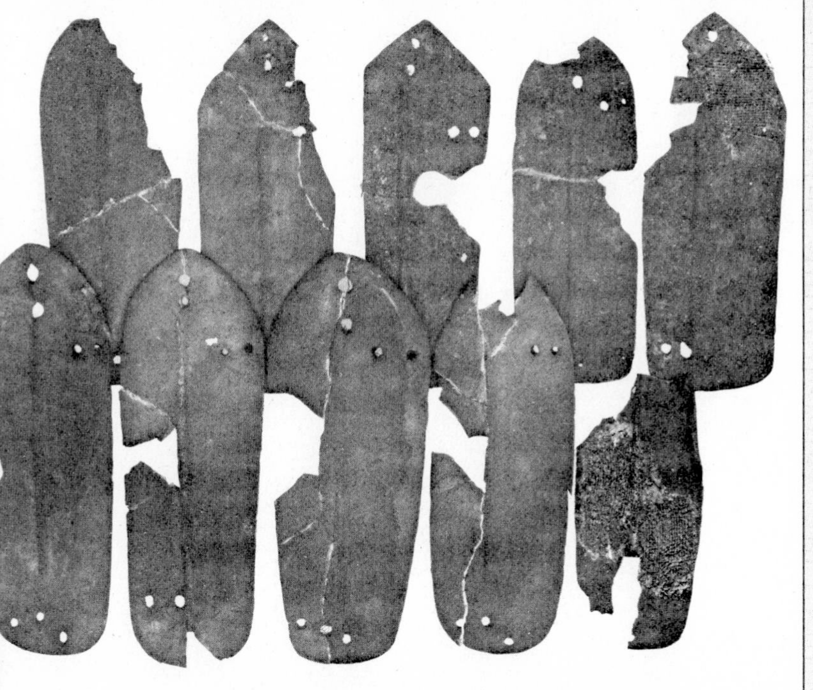

A ceremonial battle-ax in the shape of an arm (top) and pieces of bronze mail demonstrate the kind of armor and weaponry used by Hittite and Egyptian soldiers. In hand-to-hand combat the sharp-edged wrist part of the ax could slice an enemy's neck, and the thumb may have served as a hook or gouge. The mail—each piece measuring about four and a half inches long—was stitched to the soldier's garments for protection.

recover their strength and launch upon an aggressive course of action that would ultimately lead them into a headlong clash with Egypt.

When Suppiluliuma ascended to the throne in 1386 B.C., Hatti was a nation in disarray. He began his reign by restoring the decayed fortifications of Hattusa; he is credited with the construction of the great turreted wall that rimmed the southern edge of the city. And when Suppiluliuma had finished shoring up Hattusa's defenses, he turned to the bigger task at hand: reorganizing the army. His first military exploits were defensive—the repulsion of countless enemies who had taken advantage of the kingdom's weakened state and were pressing on its frontiers from the west, the north and the east. Within a few years he had his nearby adversaries in hand, and he was ready and eager to take the offensive and deal with enemies abroad.

His first foray, in 1374 B.C., was not a success. He issued his first challenge to the aggressive Mitannians. After marching nearly 300 miles with his army, he attacked the Syrian kingdom on its northwest corner, but Mitanni's troops were ready and they rebuffed him. The Hittite army suffered heavy losses in lives and equipment—and the disgrace was compounded when the Mitannian king sent part of the seized gear to his ally, the Egyptian pharaoh.

But the Hittites' shrewd general-king managed to extract from the defeat the seeds of future victory. Now he knew the lay of the land and where his adversary's defenses were strongest. He decided to approach the Mitannian problem slowly and systematically; he devised a strategy that would send his forces ranging clear across northern Syria and that would eventually cut off Mitanni from all help.

The second campaign to defeat Mitanni began in 1368 B.C. with the easy conquest of the southwestern kingdom of Nuhasse, a neighbor of Mitanni. Then Suppiluliuma waited two years before proceeding with an all-out offensive. In 1366 B.C. he took a northerly route across the Euphrates and conquered the kingdom of Isuwa in northeastern Anatolia. Then he advanced southward and threatened the Mitannian capital of Wassukanni. The southwestern kingdom of Nuhasse, already in Hittite hands, was no longer of any help to Mitanni, nor was it a passable route to the Mitannians' most powerful ally, Egypt. The situation looked hopeless to the Mitannian king and, in desperation, he fled his capital.

Suppiluliuma, now confident that there would be no interference from the Mitannians, recrossed the Euphrates and took his army on an ally-collecting tour that added seven Syrian kingdoms to the Hittite fold. The year 1366 B.C. ended with the conquest of Kadesh, a small city-state in the western part of Syria. It was a victory that would have resounding repercussions—but not in the lifetime of Suppiluliuma.

Thirteen years later, Suppiluliuma turned his attention to the few holdouts that interfered with his domination of the lands to the east and southeast of Hattusa. Most notable was the powerful and always resistant city of Carchemish. Located at a crucial trade-route junction and controlling a major ford on the Euphrates River, Carchemish was particularly attractive to the Hittites. The Hittite army took it by siege in 1353 B.C. Suppiluliuma's son, King Mursili II, later chronicled his father's military and diplomatic exploits, making special mention of the victory at Carchemish. "My father, Suppiluliuma, finally conquered the city of Carchemish. He had besieged it for seven days, and on the eighth day he fought a battle against it for one day and took it in a terrific battle. . . . When he had conquered the city . . . he removed inhabitants, utensils of silver, gold and bronze, and carried them home to Hattusa."

A curious and unprecedented incident occurred while Suppiluliuma was commanding the siege of Carchemish—an incident that could have smoothed the way for an alliance between Hatti and Egypt, but that brought them instead close to battlefield confrontation. A messenger arrived with a letter to the king from none other than Ankhesenamun, the childless and newly widowed girl-queen of Egypt's King Tutankhamen *(page 72)*. Her message was straightforward: "My husband has died, and I have no son. If you send me one of your sons, he could become my husband and a king for the country of Egypt. I will on no account accept one of my servants and make him my husband."

Suppiluliuma was flabbergasted—and more than a little skeptical of this marriage offer out of the blue. Right there, on the outskirts of Carchemish, Suppiluliuma assembled his head advisers and hastily sent off his private secretary to Egypt "to find out what truth there was in the matter with the woman." Offended at having her intentions doubted, the young queen wrote another anxious letter: "Why do you say, 'They are deceiving me?' If I had a son, would I write to a foreigner to publish my distress? You have insulted me in speaking thus. He who was my husband is dead and I have no son. I will never take one of my subjects and marry him. I have written to no one but you. Everyone says you have many sons. Give me one of them, that he may become my husband!"

It was a glorious opportunity for Suppiluliuma to

Hattusili III, the Hittite king (right), and his graceful daughter approach the palace of Ramses II, whose bride she is to become. The scene, re-created from an Egyptian stone-carved relief, includes a subtle bit of propaganda; the hands of the two royal Hittites suggest a gesture of supplication, implying—falsely, it would appear on the basis of modern scholarship—that they were paying homage to the pharaoh.

replace tacit animosity with an alliance and to put a Hittite on the throne of Egypt, but he missed the chance. The correspondence went on too long—there were at least two exchanges of letters over almost a year, and by the time he was convinced of the woman's good will and did send one of his younger sons to be her groom, an ambitious Egyptian courtier-priest had seized the widow's bed and the country's throne. When the Hittite youth arrived in Egypt, he was summarily put to death. Suppiluliuma had blundered, with consequences that would make themselves felt in Hatti half a century later, long after the king was dead.

By the time of Suppiluliuma's death, around 1348, the Hittite realm encompassed 260,000 square miles, from the west of Asia Minor bordering on the Aegean Sea as far south as the Lebanon Mountains, and from the Mediterranean coast as far inland as northern Iraq. For the first time, the Hittites' holdings rivaled those of Egypt. In fact the two empires touched each other south of Kadesh, the Syrian city-state that was to become the scene of one of history's greatest military clashes.

In 1347 B.C. Mursili II, a prince as politically shrewd and as adroit in military matters as his father, inherited the Hittite throne and empire, and successfully pursued Suppiluliuma's expansionist policies. Twenty-five years after coming to power, he passed the still-mighty empire to his son, Muwatalli. Fortunately for Hatti, Muwatalli was as gifted a monarch as had been his father and his grandfather before him. But his legacy included the old antagonism with Egypt. It fell to Muwatalli to defend, once and for all, the Hittite Empire with arms.

WILY STRATEGY AT THE BATTLE OF KADESH

The Hittites were skilled at military deception and, at the beginning of the Battle of Kadesh, tricked Ramses II into thinking they lay well beyond the city; in fact they were hiding behind it *(first map)*. Ramses raced ahead with the Amon Division, trailed by the Re, Ptah and Sutekh divisions. When he reached Kadesh, the Hittites had wheeled around to attack the Re Division *(second and third maps)*. They scattered it and then closed the trap, encircling the Amon Division *(fourth map)*.

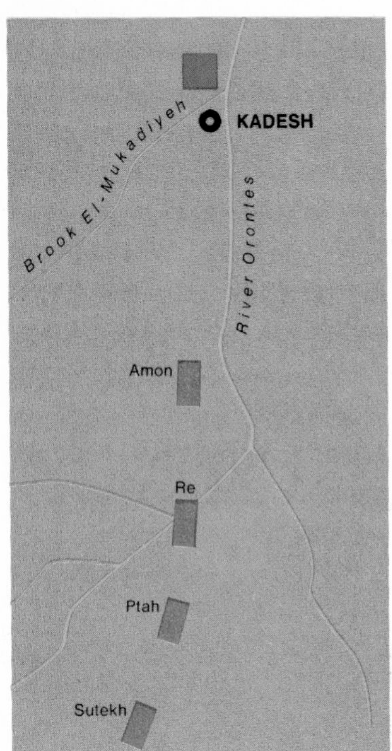

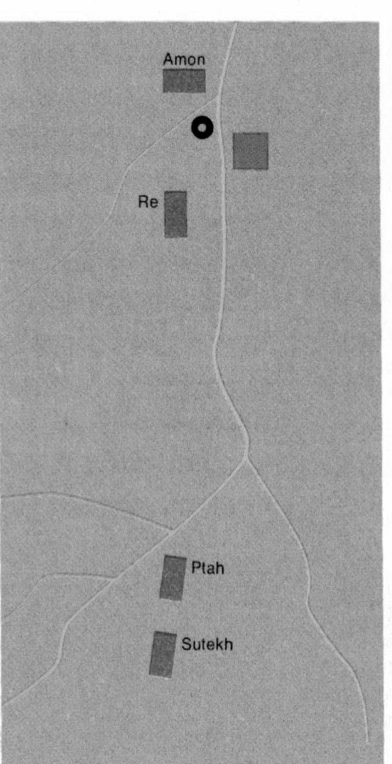

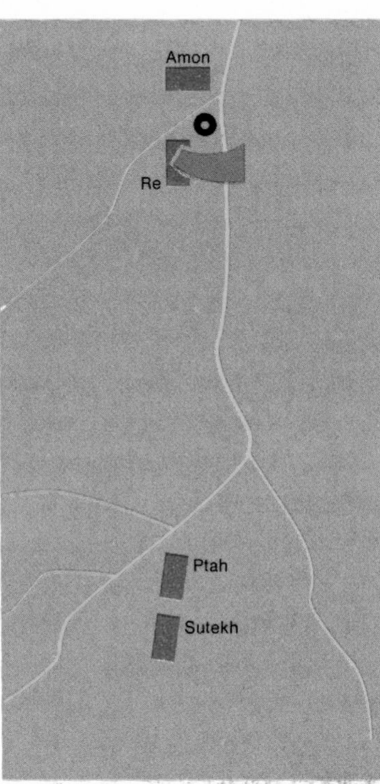

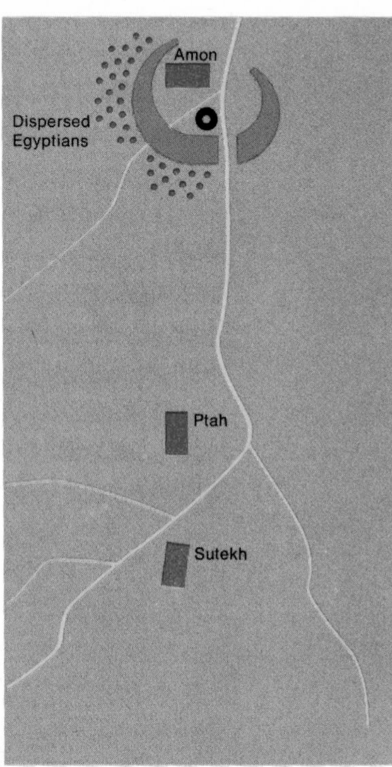

There had been minor skirmishes between the two giants before. But Egypt's own internal weakness, the product of religious upheavals and court intrigues, had kept these feuds small. Throughout the reigns of both Suppiluliuma and Mursili, Egypt had remained domestically embattled.

But in 1304 an Egyptian ruler with the courage and the military strength to challenge Muwatalli ascended the throne: Ramses II. The youthful pharaoh started his 66-year reign determined to reestablish Egyptian rule over Syria and to unseat the Hittites from their summit of power.

In 1301 B.C. Ramses hurled down the gauntlet —launching a campaign in the Hittite-held Lebanon Mountains. Muwatalli accepted the challenge readily. Egyptian records from this period tell that Muwatalli "gathered together all countries from the ends of the sea to the land of Hatti." A list of the Hittite contingents reads like a roll call of the empire. After troops from the land of Hatti itself come those from the major vassal kingdoms of Arzawa and Mitanni. Then come forces from at least six of the lesser Anatolian countries, followed by warriors from the six subject states of Syria and the southeast. Thus, an army drawn from all corners of the Hittite confederacy converged on Kadesh for what was one of the biggest battles of antiquity *(pages 83-89)*.

In the spring of 1300 B.C. two of the largest armies

that had ever been assembled met on a gravelly plain beside the Orontes River at Kadesh: the Egyptian accounts indicate that there were 40,000 troops in all. Although both rulers claimed that control of Kadesh was their purpose—two important trade routes intersected there—Kadesh itself was little more than a pretext. The real issue was status: whoever won would be supreme master of the ancient world. But the two armies and their commanders were well matched. The cunning of Muwatalli, who earned his reputation as a brilliant tactician at Kadesh *(see maps, page 80)*, was perfectly balanced by the bravery—and the good luck—of Ramses. That battle was a draw. Both generals returned to their respective capitals without a victory but with the knowledge that their contest could not be won on the battlefield.

The Battle of Kadesh was followed by just less than two decades of cold war between Hatti and Egypt; they stared at each other across the eastern end of the Mediterranean, but open war did not break out again. Relations were exacerbated by political upheaval in Hattusa. After Muwatalli's death, in 1296 B.C., a coup d'état sent his successor-son, Mursili III, scurrying for refuge; Mursili wound up in the bosom of the enemy, Egypt. When the new self-proclaimed king, Hattusili III, demanded that Mursili be returned and the Egyptian pharaoh refused, the Hittite monarch complained publicly: "When I wrote to him: send me my enemy, he did not send him, and hence I and the king of Egypt were angry with each other." But rather than go to war again, both monarchs contained their wrath.

Hattusili III was well aware, as no doubt was Ramses, that there were other possible antagonists to be faced, and so they husbanded their strength. Just across the Euphrates the king of Assyria was adding new territories to his realm and beginning to claim equal status with the Hittite and Egyptian leaders. When the Assyrian monarch referred to Hattusili III as "brother"—that is, as a political equal—and took for himself the title of Great King, Hattusili was offended. "And for what reason should I write to you about brotherhood?" he demanded of the presumptuous Assyrian. "Were you and I perhaps born of the same mother? . . . Do not write about brotherhood and Great Kingship to me."

Most likely it was a shared mistrust of Assyria's growing power that finally prompted Hattusili and Ramses to put aside their differences. In 1284, 16 years after the Battle of Kadesh, they concluded a treaty, the terms of which can still be seen inscribed on the walls of an Egyptian temple at Karnak. The treaty outlined a nonaggression, mutual-defense pact —one of the earliest of such formal diplomatic agreements between two major powers.

Not only the kings but their families were involved in the long, careful negotiations that preceded the signing of the treaty. Ramses alone sent off at least 39 letters, 26 of them to Hattusili and 13 to the Hittite queen, Puduhepa. His mother and his son, the crown prince of Egypt, also participated in the exchange of correspondence with Hattusa.

In the pact's final version, which was incised on silver tablets, the two monarchs vowed not to make war on each other, to come to each other's aid should either be attacked by a third party and to send troops in the event of internal uprising. They promised to honor the status quo of their respective frontiers and spheres of influence. Each ruler agreed to send back fugitives from the other's country (perhaps Hattusili III was recalling his rival-predecessor's flight to Egypt), but with the interesting proviso that the individuals who were extradited were not to be punished for their defection.

The bond between the new allies was further strengthened 13 years later when Ramses prepared to take a Hittite princess as his bride. So that there would be no slight, it was agreed that Hattusili's daughter would be "the Consort of the Great King, Mistress of the two Countries"—in other words, one of the pharaoh's chief wives. When Hattusili finally was satisfied with the terms, he invited Ramses to send an embassy to Hattusa "to pour fine oil on the head of my daughter, and. . .take her into the house of the Great King of Egypt!" The pharaoh wrote to his prospective mother-in-law, Queen Puduhepa, ecstatically praising "this fine decision to let these two great countries forever become one single country."

On the walls of the temple of Abu Simbel the Hittite king and his daughter can still be seen *(page 79)* approaching the enthroned pharaoh, their hands lifted in humble submission. Ramses was determined to give his subjects—and posterity—the impression that Hatti's king had made the trek all the way to Egypt for the honor of giving his daughter in marriage; there is, however, no Hittite record to confirm that Hattusili actually made the trip. But if the Egyptian account is to be believed, the Hittite princess traveled with her rich dowry in the company of an Egyptian envoy and a detachment of Hittite troops.

The Egyptian-Hittite alliance held fast for the rest of the 13th Century B.C. It was a relationship rare in that era not only for its durability, but also for the extent to which its participants helped each other. When a drought brought famine to the land of Hatti, for instance, Ramses' successor, Merneptah, shipped relief supplies of grain to Asia Minor.

The stability of the relationship with Egypt allowed other Hittite endeavors to flourish. The citizens of Hattusa could get on with the business of expanding their capital, building their great religious shrines, perfecting their laws and attending to their empire. In contrast to the many slanders about the Hittites engraved on Egyptian temple walls during the long years of struggle, one large inscription carved during the beneficent reign of Pharaoh Merneptah happily proclaimed: "Hatti is at peace."

Kadesh: A Clash of Superpowers

Hittites riding three-man chariots charge confidently into the Battle of Kadesh, as seen in a 3,200-year-old Egyptian stone relief.

One of the first recorded battles in history took place about 1300 B.C. for the city of Kadesh in northern Syria. The result was a standoff between the forces of Ramses II's mighty Egypt and the massed armies of the Hittites under King Muwatalli. There had been countless battles in many wars before this one, of course, but the Battle of Kadesh is the first about which actual strategic details are known. Despite the fact that the surviving accounts —scenes carved on temple walls, an epic poem and an official written record—are all Egyptian, calculated to publicize Ramses' personal prowess, the pharaoh permitted history to know that he had been victimized by a shrewd military ruse. Two Hittites posed as deserters and informed Ramses that Muwatalli's forces lay far north of Kadesh. The pharaoh took the spies at their word and proceeded in that direction with relaxed troops who were taken by surprise and cut to ribbons by the enemy's three-man chariots. Only their appetite for plunder diverted the Hittites long enough to make possible Ramses' successful counterattack, which recaptured the initiative from Muwatalli. Scenes on the following pages, drawn from temple reliefs, highlight aspects of the battle.

HITTITE CHARIOTS TAKE THE PHARAOH BY SURPRISE

An early stage of the Battle of Kadesh is recorded in the scene above, from a relief at Luxor. Conflict arose over increasing Hittite dominance of what the Egyptians had long considered their own sphere of influence—northern Syria. Long before Ramses II became pharaoh in 1304 B.C., the Hittites had seized Kadesh, a strategic city on the Orontes River. Ramses arrived in the north with 20,000 men in four divisions, the Amon, Re, Ptah and Sutekh. As he prepared to ford the river south of Kadesh *(map, page 13)*, the two Hittites who claimed to be deserters appeared and said that Muwatalli was at Aleppo, the capital of a Hittite ally. Actually Muwatalli, with 20,000 men including 10,500 charioteers manning 3,500 chariots, lay in wait just beyond Kadesh. Ramses and the Amon Division raced north and encamped outside the city, leaving the other divisions to follow. But "the wretched chief of Hatti," as Ramses' scribes called Muwatalli, swung his troops unseen to the flank of the Re Division and slashed through. At Ramses' camp, meanwhile, Hittite scouts who had been captured and beaten admitted that the Hittites were hiding behind Kadesh. Alarmed, Ramses sent for reinforcements. Before they arrived, however, Hittite chariots crashed into his camp. Key episodes in the Egyptian reliefs are indicated on these pages and those that follow by numbers corresponding to the captions.

1. *Seated "upon a throne of gold" in his tent in the camp northwest of Kadesh, Ramses dresses down his officers for faulty intelligence operations. Misled by his own scouts, who failed to locate the enemy, and by the false story of the Hittite "deserters," the pharaoh has rushed to Kadesh, leaving his army behind—a move he is now beginning to regret.*

2. *"The arrival of the scout of pharaoh . . . bringing the two scouts of the vanquished chief of Hatti into the presence of pharaoh" is the message in the hieroglyphic inscription adjacent to the carved scene. "They are beating them to make them tell where the wretched chief of Hatti is." In front of the victims stands Ramses' heavy-infantry guard, consisting of Egyptians (with round-topped shields) and foreign mercenaries (with circular shields and horn-crested helmets).*

3. *Ramses' camp is outlined in the relief by a rectangular barricade of shields. In its dead center stands the pharaoh's large command tent, flanked by the smaller tents of his officers. Just to the right of the tent reclines Ramses' pet lion.*

4. *Hittites in their three-man chariots smash through the shield barricade into Ramses' camp. Infantrymen of the pharaoh's camp guard, armed with short swords and spears, pull the first comers from their chariots and dispatch them. The rest of the camp is rapidly becoming aware of the surprise attack.*

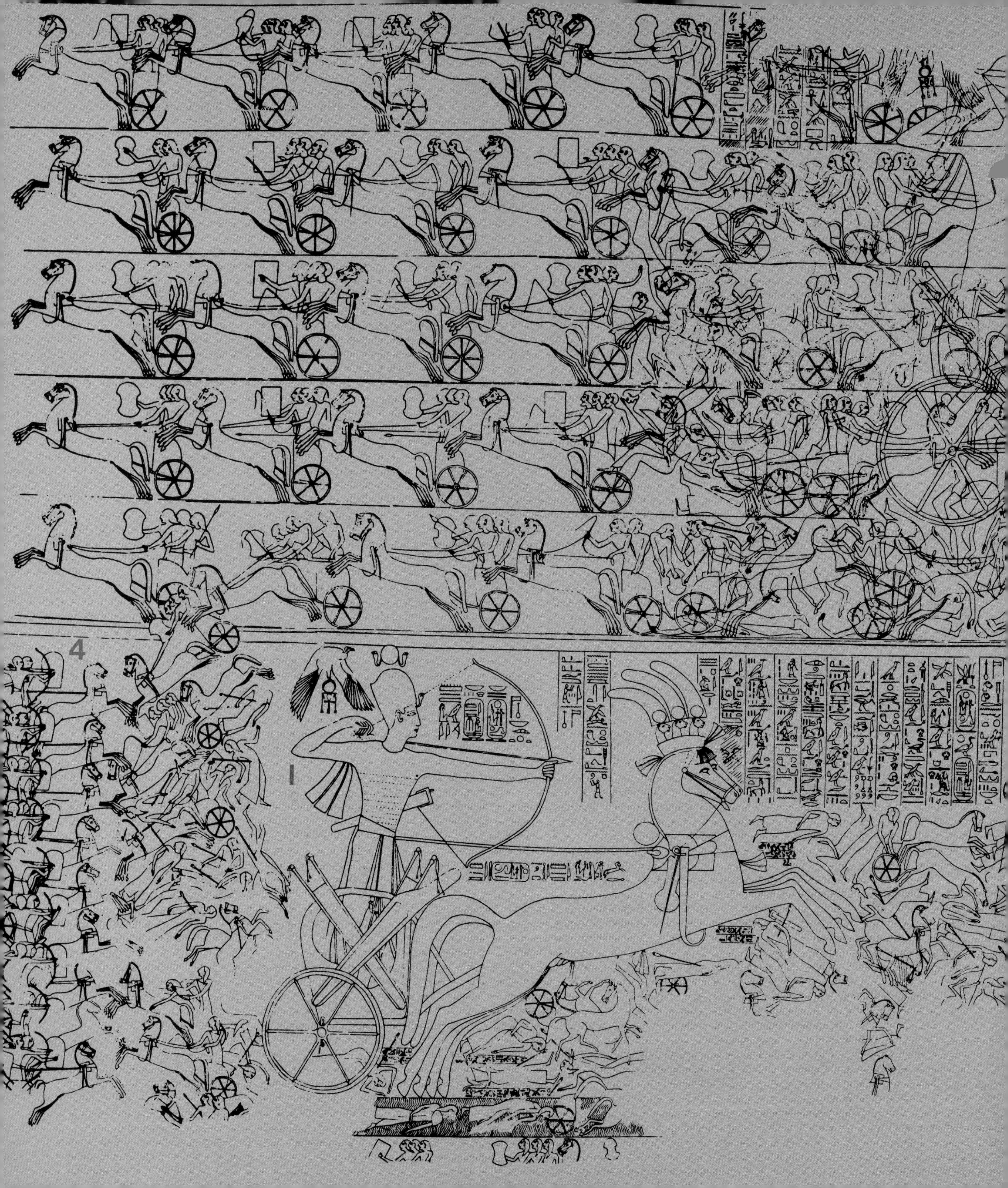
4
I

5

RAMSES' COUNTERATTACK HURLS BACK THE HITTITES

In the second stage of the battle, detailed in this scene from Thebes, Ramses responded courageously to the Hittite assault. Noting that the line of Hittite chariots encircling his camp was thin on the river side, he charged that section on his chariot. As Muwatalli looked on, surrounded by some 8,000 or 9,000 of his own infantrymen, the pharaoh drove Muwatalli's scribe, his charioteer, his bodyguard, his brother and his ally, the king of Aleppo, into the water. But Ramses soon would have been wiped out had not the Hittite charioteers dismounted to plunder the camp. Meanwhile, a fresh force of Egyptians—cryptically referred to in the reliefs as "recruits"—arrived unexpectedly and helped repel the looters.

1. *The young pharaoh attacks the foe in his war chariot. The Egyptian epic poem commemorating the battle says that Ramses "charged into the midst of the foe . . . while he was alone by himself, without another with him"—standard war-journal bombast meaning he had only a few troops.*

2. *King Muwatalli stands on the bank of the Orontes River surrounded by infantrymen. According to Egyptian texts, the Hittite king never committed himself and these soldiers to battle, despite the heavy fighting that ensued—in sharp, and presumably deliberate, contrast with Ramses' heroics.*

3. *"The wretched chief of Aleppo, turned upside down by his soldiers, after his majesty (the pharaoh) hurled him into the water," says the text. Water runs from the king's mouth.*

4. *Egyptian reinforcements come to Ramses' rescue. Evidently they are not from any of his four divisions: the reliefs call them simply "recruits from the land of Amurru" and say they "cut off the vanquished, wretched foe" and slew them.*

5. *A band of Hittite infantry, armed with short swords, stands defensively in Kadesh as the battle sweeps toward the city.*

RAMSES SNATCHES MORAL VICTORY FROM NEAR DEFEAT

Once again, in scenes of the battle's denouement as carved on a temple wall at Luxor, Ramses' personal bravery is underscored, but the city of Kadesh—to which the pharaoh's scribes always refer as "Kadesh the Deceitful"—now becomes the focus of attention.

Ramses emerged from the fighting a hero because the Hittites retreated into the fortified city after some three hours of bitter fighting. The young pharaoh displayed spectacular personal courage in combat and, with the arrival of both his "recruits" and the laggard Ptah Division, inflicted heavy casualties on the Hittite forces—but not without suffering major losses. Curiously, Muwatalli, even after he had flung in his reserve of 1,000 chariots, still did not commit all his infantry. "What made the issue a success for Ramses," one modern historian says with a touch of irony, "was his salvation from utter destruction."

The Egyptian heroic poem describing the battle indicates that there was more fighting the following day and that the Hittites sued for peace (historians agree that at worst the Hittites fought to a draw), but the reliefs stop with the Hittite flight into Kadesh. Nowhere in the official record does Ramses claim to have captured the city. For the next 16 years, in fact, he had to campaign constantly in Syria until he concluded an alliance with King Hattusili III, Muwatalli's brother.

1. *The pharaoh, galvanized into action by the Hittites' invasion of his camp, flings his chariot into a wall of Hittite chariots. Befitting his role as both pharaoh and supposed son of the sun god Re, he is portrayed looming over everyone else. The side of Ramses' chariot is adorned with the figure of an upright lion, a symbol of power and the will to fight.*

2. *An Egyptian messenger dispatched by the beset pharaoh skirts the Hittite lines to summon help from the Ptah Division marching toward Kadesh. The discovery of Muwatalli's real position on the other side of the city, the dispatch of the messenger and the incursion of the Hittite chariots into Ramses' camp probably happened almost simultaneously.*

3. *The Ptah Division arrives to join the battle. Though the fact is clear in this relief, neither the epic poem nor the official record mentions the aid supplied by the Ptah Division —perhaps because the Egyptian scribes were being careful not to appear in any way to minimize Ramses' bravery.*

4. *Well-disciplined "recruits" tear into the Hittite forces. They may have been a crack Canaanite unit of young men who had been stationed somewhere in the vicinity by the Egyptians.*

5. *Ramses and his cohorts pursue a three-man Hittite chariot right to the fortified city of Kadesh. The man closest to the chariot glances backward at a field strewn with casualties.*

Chapter Five: Roots of Greatness

The Hittite Empire may have grown mighty through war and diplomacy, but it was founded on the work of men like Tiwatapara. He conquered no territory, codified no laws, constructed no great cities. He was neither rich nor powerful nor famous, and almost certainly he could not read or write. And yet Tiwatapara represented the backbone of Hatti. Along with the bulk of the population he was a freeborn citizen; more significantly, he was a farmer.

Only with the dependable food supply provided by the fields and flocks of Tiwatapara and his fellow farmers were other men able to devote themselves to the business of empire building. Contributing a variety of specialized skills, the farmers of Hatti made possible the growth of a largely urbanized society, stabilized by a central government based on law and unified by a common belief in national gods who could be appealed to in matters of national import.

The story of Tiwatapara is recorded in a land deed inscribed in cuneiform on a clay tablet, one of thousands from the royal archives at Hattusa. The deed meticulously lists an inventory not only of his farm but of his family. He had a wife named Azzia; a boy, Haruwanduli; and two girls, Anitti and Hantawiya. They lived in "the town of Hanzusra," which probably was a village inhabited by other farmers whose fields lay in the neighborhood.

Judging from the ruins of Hittite houses unearthed by archeologists, Tiwatapara's dwelling must have been much like those still being built today in rural Anatolia—with foundations of stone or rubble, a timber framework and walls of unfired mud brick. Perhaps, if Tiwatapara's house rested on a slope, it was split-level with mud-plastered stone steps connecting its half dozen or so rooms. The floors were of hard clay, and if Tiwatapara's spouse, Azzia, was inclined to comfort or coziness, some floors may have been covered with mats of interwoven rushes.

One room was the kitchen, with a hearth and a clay oven. Another, no doubt, was a storage room where large clay crocks held supplies of wine and olive oil, and dried meat hung from the rafters. What kind of beds a Hittite farmer's family slept on is unknown, but there must have been a room or rooms for sleeping, and possibly another, with table and chairs of rough-hewn timber, that did double duty as a gathering and eating place.

Since the inventory of Tiwatapara's property mentions "one set of houses," there may have been several outbuildings, used perhaps for additional storage space or to shelter the family's livestock. Some of the animals, however, may have shared the family's quarters, as they still do in rural parts of Anatolia, providing welcome warmth in winter.

At the time his holdings were listed, Tiwatapara had six draft oxen, two other oxen (presumably for meat), 36 sheep, four lambs, 18 goats and five kids. As pasture for the oxen, he held one acre of meadowland near the neighboring town of Parkalla.

The boy Haruwanduli probably had the job of shepherding the sheep and goats as they grazed on the hillsides. Not only would he have had to guard them from wolves, but also watch that they did not damage a neighbor's property. If they wandered into

A Hittite holy family decorates a steatite mold found in the city of Kültepe in the highlands of central Anatolia. The husband, in conical hat, appears to be a storm god; the woman holding a child, a mother goddess. The mold probably was used to cast lead figures or to make impressions in clay plaques that might have served as household religious articles.

Egyptian bakers in a drawing of a tomb painting turn out various baked goods identical in shape with those described in Hittite texts. While two workers in the royal kitchen (top row) knead the dough by jumping and stamping on it, others carry some to a baker who shapes it into round, triangular and animal forms. The breads and cakes are then either deep-fried (bottom row), cooked in a pot or baked in conical clay ovens. Hittite bakers produced more than 100 different types of bread alone, some of it for ritual purposes.

the neighbor's vineyard, Tiwatapara—by Hittite law—was liable for any damage that might be done: 10 shekels of silver for each acre bearing grapes and three shekels for each acre not in fruit.

Tiwatapara's biggest asset was not his livestock, but his own three and a half acres of vineyard valued at 140 shekels. In addition, he owned 40 apple trees and 42 pomegranate trees. Tiwatapara is not credited in the deed with owning any slaves, so it is probable that he and his family tended and harvested their farm themselves.

Seasonal help was available, although it is not likely that he had need of it on such small acreage. But he may well have supplemented his own family's income by hiring out himself or his draft oxen. The fee for each was a shekel a month. And if by any chance he caught the hirer beating one of his animals with a whip, the law entitled him to claim two and a half bushels of barley in compensation. On the other hand, if his oxen strayed into a neighbor's field, the neighbor had the right to use them without paying "for one day till the stars come out."

Presumably such problems did not often arise. But there was a much bigger problem that could not be controlled by the farmers—the climate. Winters on the Anatolian plateau today produce heavy snows; summers are dry. Perhaps in Hittite times the climate was not quite so severe. Olive trees, which now are cultivated only on the coastal plains, grew in the Hittite highlands; olive oil is mentioned in Hittite records as a common commodity. There are also indications that the now almost treeless region included some areas covered by substantial forests. The ruins of Hittite buildings show that wood was a basic construction material, and cuneiform texts mention the use of oak, poplar and fir as timber.

Still, the Anatolian highlands could hardly have been a Garden of Eden. Because rains were sparse, irrigation was widely practiced, and stealing a man's water by diverting his ditch was a serious offense.

Making the best of a bad situation, Hittite farmers seem to have done quite well, and many had holdings much larger than Tiwatapara's. In addition to grapes, figs and olives, they raised barley and wheat, onions, lentils, chick peas, lettuce and beans, and—at least in some areas—flax. Beekeeping was widespread and honey was a staple product. Domesticated birds included partridges and ducks, and besides oxen, goats and sheep there were horses, asses, mules and pigs. Farmers branded their animals, but whether by searing the skin with hot metal brands or by daubing the coats with dye is not made clear in surviving texts. From Hittite laws it is known that some farm property was fenced to keep animals in—and people out. It was a greater offense to steal from a fenced vineyard than an unfenced one, and bulls had to be penned or they could be confiscated and sold by the king's court.

The farmers produced wine from their ripe grapes, oil from their olives, cheese from their goats' milk, lard from their pigs, and flour and beer from their grain. Because Tiwatapara and his fellow farmers managed to produce more food than they and their families could consume, many other Hittites never had to go near a plow and could turn to other occupations. Among these was metalworking. Anatolia had been noted for its mineral wealth even before the Hittites made it their homeland. Copper had long been the major export of the Assyrian merchants who established their *karums*, or trading colonies, outside

Anatolian cities in pre-Hittite days. Iron ore, also, was plentiful. The Hittites apparently held a monopoly on the production of iron; even so, it was for them a rare and expensive metal. Only a few Hittite metalworkers knew how to create the high temperatures necessary for smelting iron ore. The widespread notion that Hittites plunged into battle wielding iron swords that could smash the weapons of softer metal used by their enemies is not founded on fact. Their smiths did indeed fashion some swords of iron, as well as thrones, ornaments and statues of gods, but most of these objects were either ensconced in temples as gifts for gods or given as royal presents to foreign rulers.

Although iron was as costly as gold in Hittite times, its hardness made it particularly attractive to those who could afford the metal, and apparently Hittite kings were sometimes asked by other monarchs to send them quantities of it. "As for the good iron which you wrote about to me," replied a Hittite ruler of the 13th Century B.C. to such a request by another monarch, probably the king of Assyria, "good iron is not available in my seal-house in Kizzuwatna. That it is a bad time for producing iron I have written. They will produce good iron, but as yet they will not have finished. When they have finished I shall send it to you. Today now I am dispatching an iron dagger blade to you."

Silver was in greater supply, enough so that it was used as the basic medium of exchange. Cast in bars or rings, it was measured out by weight; 40 shekels equaled one mina of silver, and if the Hittite currency corresponded to Babylonian values, 60 minas equaled one talent. Lead served for currency of less worth; it was used as well for container lids and combs for carding wool or flax. Tin was mixed with copper in the production of bronze, and by itself was highly prized as a plating.

Besides supporting the workers who mined and fashioned such metals, Hittite agriculture also sustained a great many other specialists, among them leather craftsmen, cobblers, weavers, fullers, potters, basketmakers, carpenters, stonemasons, merchants, priests, physicians and scribes. Some of these workers must have organized themselves into pressure groups, if not full-fledged guilds or unions. That such organizations existed is suggested by text references to men of certain occupations complaining to the king that other categories were being excused from the occasional conscripted labor demanded by the state.

If common labor sustained the empire, it was law that held it together. In nearly all aspects of Hittite life—on the farm of Tiwatapara and on those of his neighbors, in the mines, in the homes and workshops of craftsmen, even in the palace of the king himself—the rule of law was supreme. The royal archives have yielded 200 statutes, many of which apparently were based on judgments in specific cases, somewhat as modern laws have derived from "precedents." Hittitologists believe that, in addition to these written laws, there probably existed a body of unwritten laws—in effect, common law.

Hittite law not only regulated much social conduct, but also permeated economic activities to a degree that some present-day businessmen might find obnoxious. It even delineated what is one of history's first statutory price-and-income controls, although it is not known how rigidly the prescribed wages and prices were enforced.

For example, the price of a blue woolen garment was pegged by law at 20 shekels of silver and that of a fine shirt at three shekels. Two cheeses should cost one shekel; one tub of oil, two shekels. And if a man hired himself out for the full three months of harvest, undertaking to "bind the sheaves . . . get onto the wagon . . . bring it into the barn . . . and clear the threshing floor," he would be paid 75 bushels of barley. A woman hiring herself out for the harvest for two months was paid only 30 bushels.

This marked discrepancy in wages does not mean that the Hittites were altogether antifeminist. While Hittite society was patriarchal, the law guaranteed to women certain rights that put them several notches above the status of mere chattels assigned to women in some ancient societies. A girl could break an engagement and marry another man, even without her parents' consent, as long as the jilted fiancé got back his betrothal gift and the new husband paid to her parents the traditional bride price. A widowed mother could disinherit her son if he failed to support her in old age. In divorce, a woman could claim custody of some of her children. And at the highest level of society, the Hittite queens enjoyed special powers that in some cases equaled the authority of their husbands. They conducted their own diplomatic correspondence and retained their titles and prerogatives after their spouses' death. While the old queen was still alive, the woman married to the new monarch was known only as the king's wife.

On the whole, Hittite law was more humane than other ancient codes, certainly more so than the Babylonian Code of Hammurabi (according to which even a simple theft was punishable by death), and in some respects more so than the laws of the Israelites. It was calculated to compensate fairly the victim of a crime as well as to inflict retribution on the wrongdoer, and thus dissuaded the offended party or his family from seeking revenge.

An arsonist, for instance, was required to rebuild

the house he had burned. A murderer might be required to recompense the family for their loss or face death, but the death penalty could be inflicted only at the discretion of the heirs. The mandatory death penalty was reserved for refusal to submit to the authority of the king, for certain forms of bestiality and for rape—but only in those cases where "a man seizes a woman in the mountains." If he took her instead in her home and she did not shout for help, the charge was not rape but adultery. And if her husband found the pair, the law said he could not be punished for killing them both on the spot. If he chose to spare his wife, however, he had to spare the man as well.

Slaves also enjoyed statutory protection. Their marriages to free men and women were recognized and had legal status. If a freeman cohabited with a slave woman and later threw her out, she had the right to take one of their children.

Little is known about Hittite courts. On the local level judicial responsibility seems to have been shared between the elders of a town and the provincial garrison commander acting as the king's representative. The elders probably settled what disputes they could, saving for the commander's attention those cases in which one or both parties remained unsatisfied. Acting as a judge appears to have been one of the main duties of this officer, who was repeatedly admonished to be unbiased in his rulings. "Summon forth all the people of the city," he was instructed. "Whoever has a suit, decide it for him and satisfy him. If the slave of a man, or the maidservant of a man, or a bereaved woman has a suit, decide it for them and satisfy them."

If he found a case too involved for his judgment, the garrison commander referred it to the highest court in the land—the king himself. Certain cases, such as those involving the practice of sorcery or those in which the accused was liable to execution, automatically went to the king.

While there are no records that show ordinary tribunals in action, accounts of special inquiries dealing with matters of state do exist, and they indicate that great efforts were made to determine the truth. Some of these proceedings read like transcripts of Washington's livelier congressional hearings. One relates an inquiry into the conduct of a man named Great-is-the-Storm-God, who was accused of illegally disposing of some of the queen's property, including livestock that had been entrusted to him. After sworn testimony had been heard from witnesses, the defendant was questioned.

"One pair of mules you gave to Hillarizzi," charged one of his accusers. Great-is-the-Storm-God denied they were the queen's mules: "The mules belonged to Hillarizzi; I . . . gave them back safe and sound." Another accuser broke in at this point to say that one of Great-is-the-Storm-God's men was involved in selling a horse belonging to the queen "and got a talent of bronze." As if he were profoundly shocked at hearing this information, Great-is-the-Storm-God answered: "My man told me it had died!"

The fate of the defendant is not known; after further testimony the account breaks off in mid-hearing. But as Professor O. R. Gurney states in his book *The Hittites,* texts like these demonstrate "a spirit of careful and unbiased investigation which may perhaps be taken as typical of Hittite administration as a whole." However, when the court was faced by contradictory testimony, it was not above resorting to a

A Splendid Inheritance

When the Hittites first settled in Asia Minor, they became beneficiaries of the indigenous culture that was already flourishing there. Striking evidence of some of the things to which the newcomers fell heir has emerged from excavations at Kanesh, a busy trading center when the Hittites arrived around 2000 B.C. The site has revealed that spacious, two-story houses lined well-laid-out streets and public squares. At least two buildings near the market area may have served as restaurants; they contained unusual amounts of pottery, perhaps used for cooking and serving food.

The market was an exchange place for goods brought from abroad by Assyrian merchants, who left behind on clay tablets the earliest written records yet found in Anatolia. And so skilled were the potters of Kanesh that their fine wares *(right)* were rarely excelled during even the greatest days of the Hittite Empire.

Elegant but practical, this 16-inch-tall pitcher has knobs in front, which provided a grip for the pourer's other hand.

This libation vessel in the shape of a growling lion has a spout on its back. It measures only eight inches high.

Some six inches long, this head of a ram, whose eyes were once inlaid, may have been part of a vase or drinking cup.

trial by ordeal and having both parties tossed into a river. The one who floated was presumed to be telling the truth.

The fairness of any government depends greatly on that of the man at its head. This is especially true if his power is absolute or nearly so, as was that of Hittite monarchs after the demise of the *pankus*, the assembly of nobles that in pre-empire days had acted as a counterweight to royal authority.

On the whole, the Hittite rulers seem to have been men of conscience and honor. But however much they may have been respected by the populace, they had to be on guard against palace coups, and at times they were ruthless. Labarna II (the king who made Hattusa the Hittite capital and changed his name accordingly to Hattusili, "the man from Hattusa") discovered his own appointed heir, a nephew also named Labarna, leading a conspiracy to overthrow him. Hattusili furiously condemned this treachery before the assembled dignitaries in a speech that is one of the most vibrant examples of Hittite oratory:

"The young Labarna I had proclaimed to you saying 'He shall sit upon the throne.' I, the king, called him my son, embraced him, exalted him, and cared for him continually. But he showed himself a youth not fit to be seen: he shed no tears, he showed no pity, he was cold and heartless. I, the king, summoned him to my couch and said: 'Well! No one will in future bring up the child of his sister as his foster-son!' . . . Enough! He is my son no more! Then his mother bellowed like an ox." Hattusili named another successor. "Behold, Mursili is now my son," he said. "In place of the lion the god will set up another lion."

After a long and successful reign, Mursili himself

The law of the land is inscribed in tidy cuneiform script on a fragment of a clay tablet found in the royal archives at Hattusa. One law, in the second section above, reads: "If anyone finds an ox, sheep, horse or ass, he shall drive it back to its owner and (the owner) shall reward him." Such down-to-earth practicality typified Hittite jurisprudence.

was assassinated by a brother-in-law, who then became king. This was the beginning of a dismal series of palace plots, coups and murders that was ended only by passage of an enlightened law. King Telipinu, who succeeded to the throne about 1525 B.C., observed the debilitating effect upon the state of all this plotting and remarked with regret that "in Hattusa bloodshed has become common." Telipinu —though he himself had seized the throne and eliminated other contenders by force—decided to put a stop to the bloody business once and for all:

"Let a prince, the son of a wife of the first rank, be king. If there is no prince of the first rank, let one who is a son of the second rank become king. If, however, there is no prince, let them take a husband for a daughter of the first rank and let him become king."

Telipinu's law of succession somehow did the trick. It brought a new atmosphere of stability not only to the Hittite kingship but to the nation as a whole. There was not another coup for 200 years.

A Hittite king must have been a very busy man. In addition to being chief judge, he was his own chief diplomat and chief priest. To assist him, he had a palace staff of officers, usually his relatives, with such titles as chief of the courtiers, chief of the treasurers, chief of the "overseers of 1,000," chief of the scepter bearers and chief of the bodyguard.

The king's role as commander-in-chief of the army could not be delegated. It was impossible to sit on the throne in Hattusa and oversee the far-flung activities of generals in the field. Campaigning began in the spring with the melting of the deep snows in the Hittite homeland, and generally continued throughout the summer months. During a good part of that time the monarch almost invariably led campaigns in person. In the autumn he would hurry back to Hattusa to deal with diplomatic correspondence, hand down decisions on legal cases and consult with the city's governor on the administration of the capital before departing with his entourage on his winter tour of provincial cities.

This annual trek probably served a political function, allowing the king a firsthand check on government in the provinces and allowing the country in turn to see the king. But its main purpose was religious. As high priest, the king visited all the major shrines and conducted festivals in honor of the leading gods. During this pilgrimage, he, his queen and the crown prince sojourned at royal palaces scattered throughout the land. No remains of these palaces have been found, however, and some may have been no more than lavish villas.

On tour or in residence at Hattusa, the king had no responsibilities more important than his religious commitments. To neglect them might cause the gods to turn their backs on him, and the whole country would suffer the consequences. A serious national emergency would find him on the roof of his palace before two tables stacked with loaves of sacrificial bread, saying the special prayer reserved for those occasions "when things get too much for a man." "The bird takes refuge in its nest and lives," he would pray. "I have taken refuge with the Storm God . . . so save my life! . . . Walk on my right hand! Team up with me as a bull to draw the wagon!"

As spring began to smile on the Anatolian plateau and as the king celebrated his last religious festival at Hattusa, it was again time to mobilize his army and prepare for another season of campaigning. On

Found buried next to each other in the ruins of Hattusa's citadel, these 36-inch-tall terra-cotta bulls are neatly matched from the tips of their lyre-shaped horns to the markings on their bodies. Archeologists speculate that they represent Sheri and Hurri, the twin bulls that drew the Storm God's chariot.

such a strenuous schedule, it is a wonder that things did not get "too much for a man" more often than they did. And it is understandable that Hittite monarchs, for all their devotion to their religious responsibilities, adopted the practice of saying their routine daily prayers by proxy, assigning a scribe to read them to the gods.

Just as law helped guide and direct the Hittites, so religion motivated them. And yet, however religious they may have been, the common people occasionally must have found—just as the king did—that the demands of frequent worship were a nuisance. There were simply so many gods requiring elaborate ritualistic homage. Temple officials were expressly enjoined not to let a person get away with excuses: "If he embraces your knees saying, 'Do me a favor and let me finish (my) business first. But when that business of mine is finished I shall perform the festival as prescribed,' do not yield to a man's whim, let him not take precedence over the gods."

By far the largest number of tablets recovered from the royal archives deal with religious matters. They describe a great many festival rites, outline the duties of priests and laymen, provide lengthy accounts of the questioning of oracles and—most fascinating—relate myths that give some insight into the development of the Hittite pantheon and the behavior of its divine occupants.

The Hittite gods were many. Most had been taken over from other peoples as the kings of Hattusa built the empire. By late imperial times the gods whose influence weighed most were those adopted from the Hurrians, a neighboring people who had been partly absorbed into the empire.

As might be expected in a land so severely treated by climate, the deity most commonly worshiped by the Hittites was the Storm God, known by his Hurrian name, Teshub. This tempestuous character (usually pictured holding a mace but sometimes grasping a lightning bolt) thundered above the mountains in a chariot pulled by his sacred bulls, Sheri and Hurri *(page 100)*. Although the Storm God was called the King of Heaven, the leading figure in the Hittite state religion was his wife, the Sun Goddess, a deity who had been fused with a similar Hurrian goddess called Hebat. A Hittite monarch with problems would seek her help before that of any other deity. The Hittites referred to her as "Queen of the land of Hatti, Queen of Heaven and Earth, mistress of the kings and queens of the land of Hatti, directing the government of the King and Queen of Hatti."

This melting together of divine personalities taken over from various peoples naturally casts confusion on any attempt to survey the Hittite pantheon systematically. There was, for instance, a sun god named Istanu who was mentioned in myths and cited in treaties as king of the gods and supreme patron of justice, yet he seems to have been much less important than the Storm God. Among other deities the Hittites adopted as their own and elevated to national prominence were Kushukh, the Hurrian moon god; Ea, the god of subterranean waters, who was imported from Mesopotamia via the Hurrians; and the great Babylonian deity Ishtar, a goddess whom the Hittites knew as Shaushka and among whose main concerns were matters of love and sex.

Hittite gods were not remote, majestic figures. In the myths that were recited during their festivals they complain, cheat, lie, threaten, fight, bear grudges and frequently lose their tempers as any mortal Hittite must have done. Consider, for example, the human frailties and emotions shown in one recital of the struggle for the kingship of heaven.

Once, "in the olden days," a god named Alalu was king of heaven and, as long as he held the throne, another god, Anu, would show respect and "sink at his feet and set the drinking cup in his hand." One day this apparently faithful servant rose against his master and seized the throne for himself. He in turn was served his drinking cup by the god Kumarbi, the son of Alalu. Under the circumstances Anu might well have been suspicious of his own cupbearer, but Kumarbi caught him unawares and grabbed him "by his feet and dragged him down from the sky."

Kumarbi made a mistake, however. Not a clean fighter even by the standards of Hittite gods, he bit off and swallowed Anu's genitals, after which he "rejoiced and laughed," but only until Anu pointed out that he was now impregnated with the seeds of several "dreadful gods." Some of these Kumarbi managed to spit out onto the earth: one became the River Tigris and another became Tashmishu, an advisor to Teshub. But the third, the Storm God, grew in Kumarbi's belly and caused his host no little distress by wondering aloud which of Kumarbi's orifices he should use as an exit.

Once born—he chose to emerge from Kumarbi's "good place," whatever that may have been—Teshub gave battle to Kumarbi. The details of the fight have not come down to us (the tablet on which the tale is recorded is broken at this point), but the Storm God must have won because he is next found reigning as king of heaven while Kumarbi plots a way to recover his throne.

Kumarbi's inspiration came in the form of a huge

Standing less than two inches tall, this 3,500-year-old Anatolian seal (two sides and the base are pictured here) is carved with minute scenes of unidentified rituals. All five facets were incised and could be pressed into soft clay to mark goods or legal documents. By threading a cord through the perforated handle the owner could carry the seal around his neck.

rock that he seemed to think looked like a woman. ("His desire was aroused and he slept with the rock. His manhood flowed into her; five times he took her . . . ten times he took her . . .") This unlikely union produced Ullikummi, a lad whose body was diorite and who, when placed in the sea, displayed a growth rate that would make any parent beam with pride. Before long he was 9,000 leagues tall and causing general consternation among the gods.

When the Storm God saw Ullikummi, he was frightened to tears by the new challenger and cried aloud, "Who can bear to look on so vexatious a sight? Who will dare go and battle?" Finally the Storm God screwed up his courage, hitched his bulls to his chariot (after first anointing their horns with oil and plating their tails with gold), called in 70 other gods and some storm clouds for assistance and did battle with his huge rival. Despite all his preparations he lost the first round to Ullikummi.

The Hittite myths are rich with details enhancing the narrative. The Sun Goddess, on learning of her husband's defeat, was so badly unnerved that she "barely missed falling from the roof" on which she was standing awaiting news. The myth tellers also had a sense of humor. Ubelluri, a Hittite god who presaged the function of Atlas by holding the heavens on his shoulders, was unaware that the new giant Ullikummi was up there too, adding his weight to the burden. When he was informed, he replied—no doubt in a long-suffering tone of voice—"When they built heaven and earth upon me I did not know anything. When they came and severed the heaven from the earth with a cleaver, I did not know that either." But now that Ullikummi was mentioned, he did notice that "my right shoulder is a little sore."

With the help of Ea, the Mesopotamian god of subterranean waters, an older, wiser god who commanded much respect—even the Storm God had to bow 15 times to him just to say hello—Ullikummi was finally defeated. This was done by severing the monster's feet from the shoulder of Ubelluri with the same cleaver that had been used to separate heaven and earth. Further details of the conflict are lost in the tablet's obliterated lines, but in the end the Storm God remained king of heaven. A different account of this tale appears on page 132.

In Hittite mythology this was a difficult position to maintain. The heavenly ruler was forever being challenged. In one important myth—of which two versions are preserved—his opponent is Illuyanka, a dragon. As one version of the story opens, the dragon has already stolen the Storm God's heart and eyes. To get even, the god sires a son by a mortal woman and sends him to marry the dragon's daughter. Since it was customary for the bride's parents to give a gift to a son-in-law, who came to live with them, the Storm God instructs his son to ask for the god's heart and eyes. Unwilling to refuse a request from a new son-in-law, the dragon Illuyanka hands them over. His powers restored, the Storm God promptly attacks Illuyanka. Just as he is about to deliver the deathblow, his son shouts up to him (apparently in a fit of remorse for having betrayed his father-in-law's hospitality): "Count me as with him! Spare me not." So the Storm God obligingly kills both. Another version of this myth is told on page 134.

In one version or another, this myth was recited every spring as part of the rituals surrounding one of the major events on the Hittite canonical calendar, the *purulli* festival. *Purulli* means "of the earth" and since the Hittite year began in the spring, it is possible that this occasion was the Hittites' New Year festival, with the Storm God's victory over the dragon representing the rebirth of the earth. In addition to the rites required in the worship of their numerous gods, the Hittites had other rituals for working or counteracting magic. A superstitious people, they took sorcery as seriously as they did religion—so seriously that they had laws prohibiting the careless practice of it. For example, if a man completed a certain purification rite and dropped the remnants of the rite in someone else's field or house, he was believed to have contaminated the other person's property, and the case was considered grave enough to require the king's own judgment.

In fact, so plentiful and elaborate were their magic rituals *(pages 102-113)*—designed to deal with the problems ranging from pestilence to sexual impotence—that one almost wonders how the Hittites found time to conduct their normal affairs. One ritual, to reconcile husband and wife after a family quarrel, involved not only a great many incantations by a sorceress (called the Old Woman in the ancient cuneiform texts), but also involved more than 50 distinct operations, as well as a phenomenal number of props. These included such commodities as salt, mutton fat, wax, wine, oil, dough, honey, figs, raisins, several substances the names of which scholars have not yet translated, wool (in three colors: black, red, and blue), a pig, three sheep and the horn of an ox.

The prospect of going through this daunting marathon of a rite must have deterred more than one Hittite couple on the verge of a shouting match, both because the price of the necessary livestock came high and because it required such tiresome business as digging holes in which to bury the animals after they had been sacrificed. Only the pig and two of the sheep were killed, by the way. "One white sheep they do not kill . . . the Old Woman gets it." The Old Woman, of course, wrote the instructions.

Even if the Old Woman's canniness were not in itself evidence to the contrary, the intellectual development of the Hittites should not be gauged by their adherence to superstitious practices. Only a creative, thoughtful people could have produced their successful economy, their enlightened law and their effective system of government. And only such a people could have built as formidable a city as Hattusa.

Folk Rites to Purify, Protect and Punish

Given the Hittites' passion for order and legality, ritual observances figured in every aspect of daily life. There were, of course, the formal festivals and holy events, celebrated in temples and sanctuaries by the priests of the state religion, centered in Hattusa. But there were also countless other ceremonies conducted in the open air by members of an unofficial but highly revered lay priesthood. The folk rites governed domestic affairs and friendship, prosperity and health, even the enforcement of law. The presiding personages were usually the wise old men or women of the towns and villages in outlying parts of the empire, and the populace honored them for their supposed ability in communicating with a wide range of supernatural forces.

With their prayers and incantations, the people (a) sought the things they wished for, (b) secured with offerings what they already possessed and (c) bound their agreements with oaths. Though the ceremonies often took place in informal locations and no special dress was worn, the rites were as rigidly prescribed and as meticulously followed as a high mass.

Some 70 texts, elaborating in minute detail how Hittite rituals were conducted, have been recovered from archeological sites. On this page and those that follow, selected passages from those texts accompany an artist's impressions of the rites.

In a purification rite, a country priestess and four male attendants prepare to lower a miniature boat into a channel leading to a river; the vessel's cargo is a symbolic load of sins and curses. Two of the attendants hold a pitcher and a jug from which the priestess will pour honey and oil into the stream after the boat is launched. As part of the ceremony, the priestess will recite a prayer: "Just as the river has carried away the ship and no trace of it can be found any more, whoever has committed evil word, oath, curse and uncleanliness in the presence of the god—even so let the river carry them away! And just as no trace of the ship can be found any more, let evil word no longer exist for my god."

A priestess strings a cord over a client and intones to the spirits: "Loosen the evil tension of his head, his hands and his feet. Give it to the wicked adversaries! But to the sacrificers give life, vigor and long years!" From the woman sacrificer's wrist, she takes a bowstring tied to a scrap of tin and winds it around a mouse (opposite). Before releasing the mouse, she declares: "I have taken the evil off you and transferred it to this mouse. Let this mouse carry it on a long journey to the high mountains, hills and dales!"

A Ritual to Banish Worldly Woes

To rid themselves of problems such as ill health, apprehensions or troubles believed to be curses inflicted by enemies, "sacrificers"—that is, people who sought relief from their difficulties—went through a prolonged and enormously complex rite. Like so many other Hittite rituals, this one was conducted by an old woman. Probably in return for a fee, either in goods or in currency, she provided the proper incantations and the great array of required paraphernalia.

The ceremony, which must have taken several days to perform, called for pine cones, a tree and several pieces of wood, fur, semiprecious stones, six different metals, loaves of bread—both baked and unbaked—wine and several animals, alive as well as butchered.

For the portion of the ceremony illustrated on these pages, the priestess needed a long cord, a bowstring, dough shaped into balls, a bit of tin and a live mouse. The Hittite text is explicit to the minutest detail: "She takes a cord," it prescribes, "and strings it from the sacrificers' feet to their heads on either side. She also strings it down their backs."

The ceremony was intended to accomplish three things at the same time: first, to enlist the aid of helpful spirits; second, to banish harmful ones; and finally to transmit the sacrificers' troubles to the lives of their enemies—who deserved them.

Inviting and Dismissing the Gods

The Hittites saw their gods and goddesses as omnipotent but also flawed; like humans, Hittite deities had as many faults as they did virtues. They could be vicious, jealous, vengeful, greedy or just plain forgetful; and when they were forgetful, the people who worshiped them suffered hunger, sorrow and poverty.

To woo back remiss gods—gods thought to have turned their backs on the land of Hatti—Hittite diviners conducted a lengthy, strenuous ritual. They addressed the straying deities with wailing and prayers, and they tried to tempt them home with generous offerings of the finest foodstuffs. Illustrated at right is the ceremony that was followed to recover the attentions of the Cedar gods—beneficent deities of a richly forested southern coastal area.

The Hittites often blamed the gods of their enemies for their own troubles. The drawing on the opposite page illustrates a rite devised by a priest called Uhhamuwa to rid his homeland of pestilence. The tone and actions of the rite expressed esteem—all deities, including those of the enemy, were accorded proper respect. Even so the rite's intent is plain: to put an end to the pestilence by transmitting it via a foreign god to his own worshipers—citizens of an unidentified but presumably hostile nation, whom the Hittites regarded as the plague's rightful victims.

A diviner tries to lure home errant gods by fanning the air with an eagle wing and crying mournfully. Another sprinkles libations onto trails of honey, flour and a mixture of oil and wine; the trails lead to an altar set up with food for the neglectful gods. The third diviner, meanwhile, tries to cajole the gods with prayer: "Wherever ye may be, O Cedar gods, whether in heaven or on earth, whether on mountains or in rivers, whether in the Mitanni country or . . . in the Kaska country . . . come ye now back to the Hatti land!"

Crowned with a wreath woven of blue, red, yellow, white and black wool yarn, a captured ram heads for the hills—the home of foreign gods—urged by the proddings of troubled Hittites. The ram's headdress symbolizes a pestilence that has gripped them. "Whatever god of the enemy land has caused this plague," they pray, "See! We have now driven up this crowned ram to pacify thee! Just as a city wall is strong but makes peace with the battering ram, do thou, the god who has caused this plague, make peace with Hatti!"

Ceremonies to Make Domestic Peace

Hittites employed rites to help solve their personal problems, and especially to end arguments. Just as a family counselor serves troubled people in the modern world, so the priestess Mastigga served some Hittites in the 14th Century B.C. Mastigga—as one ancient clay tablet reveals—practiced her art of easing strained family relations in the kingdom of Kizzuwatna, a onetime Hittite subject nation near the Mediterranean coast, some 175 miles south of Hattusa.

The prayers the priestess Mastigga recited and the ceremonial activities she performed were designed to settle feuds and establish peace between husbands and wives, parents and their children, and siblings. Thus when quarreling parties were not able to resolve their disputes on their own, they went, usually in pairs, to seek Mastigga's conciliatory aid.

At the sacrificers' request, Mastigga drew out and destroyed their contentious words, much as a doctor or a healer would treat a patient with a bodily infection. The Hittites, like many other ancient peoples, believed that mental grievances took palpable form and thus could be excised physically. Three of the peacemaking rituals she and others like her performed are illustrated here.

A quarrelsome couple watches as the priestess Mastigga burns a symbolic package in the shape of a tongue, representing hostile words. As the packages, made of wool wrapped in mutton fat, splutter in the flames, she recites: "Whatever thou spokest with thy mouth and tongue . . . let it be cut out of your body these days!"

Subdued by a priestess' assistant, a white sheep serves as the receptacle for the ill will between brothers. As the priestess instructs, "Spit ye out those evil curses!" the brothers prepare to spit into the sheep's open mouth. The sheep will be slaughtered and then buried to put the curses to rest.

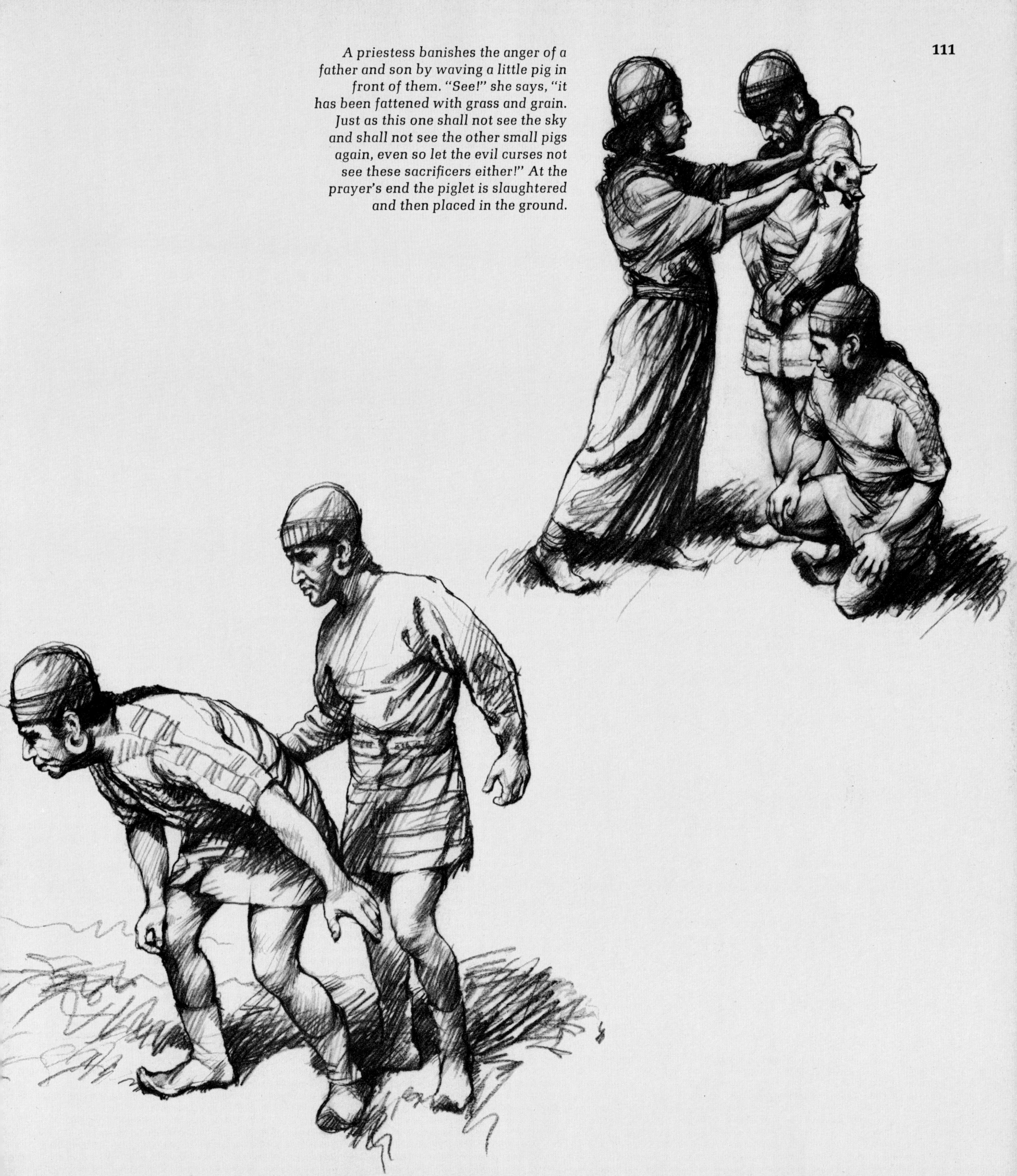

A priestess banishes the anger of a father and son by waving a little pig in front of them. "See!" she says, "it has been fattened with grass and grain. Just as this one shall not see the sky and shall not see the other small pigs again, even so let the evil curses not see these sacrificers either!" At the prayer's end the piglet is slaughtered and then placed in the ground.

A Soldier's Vow and a Peasant's Punishment

Obedience to the law of the land was the most serious of all duties for the Hittites; they were ritually bound to their agreements and obligations and if they failed to live up to them, they could pay severely.

To ensure that an army recruit would serve faithfully, for example, he was sworn in with the ceremony illustrated below. The soldiers' oath concerned itself more with threat than with instruction; it was assumed that a man knew—or would learn quickly enough—how to obey the orders of his commanding officers. The text then spelled out in explicit terms the various penalties for disloyalty, including blindness, deafness and—perhaps worst of all from the point of view of a Hittite (or any other) soldier—being turned into a woman.

Hittite courts determined guilt or innocence by listening to testimony and weighing the evidence. If the judges found a person guilty, the criminal underwent punishment, including some of a ritualistic nature. A pair of clay tablets spells out in detail a full 200 provisions for handling all conceivable crimes and misdemeanors, from murder to the theft of a beehive. The terrible price a man paid for defying the king—one of the gravest of crimes, in the Hittite view of things—is illustrated opposite. The wrongdoer did not pay by himself for the crime he had committed; all the members of his immediate family, including the elders and even the littlest children, suffered the same punishment.

Two robed priests and a priestess swear two recruits into the army. Although the inductees already have their battle helmets and boots, they are now receiving arrows that will be broken, and women's trappings, symbols of the disgrace they will endure if they shirk their duties. If they are disloyal, says one of the priests, "Let them dress them in the fashion of women! . . . Let them break the bows, arrows and clubs in their hands and let them put in their hands distaff and mirror!"

Found guilty of disobeying the king, a peasant gathers his family and stands by their home as law-enforcement officers dismantle the house. According to Hittite law, "If anyone rejects the judgment of the king, his house shall be made a heap of rubble." Scholars interpret the word "house" to mean "household" and infer that in cases of defiance to the king not only was the building destroyed but the culprit and his closest relatives as well—probably by stoning.

Chapter Six: A Walk through Hattusa

Modern archeological evidence indicates that Hattusa, the great imperial capital, probably began as two small hamlets that were founded about 2000 B.C., when the region was part of the native Anatolian kingdom of Hatti. Both stood within the area that the Hittites would ultimately surround with city walls —a spur of land sloping down in a northerly direction, bounded on the east by a precipitous gorge and on the west by a deep valley.

One hamlet was built on a rocky prominence (now known as Büyükkale, meaning "big castle"), where centuries later Hittite kings were to erect their fortified palaces. The motive of the pre-Hittite settlers in choosing this location obviously was the ease of defense offered by its high elevation. The other hamlet was on a natural terrace that lay at the foot of the northwestern slope of the same prominence. The second site was closer to the seven springs that blessed both early communities with reliable sources of water year in and year out.

Most of the ruins of these early hamlets were found beneath layers of construction piled up by successive generations of inhabitants. The remains of a pre-Hittite house excavated on Büyükkale offer proof that the villages were not primitive. Whoever owned the residence must have been a person of great means. The house measured more than 60 by 50 feet and had eight or more rooms, on several levels, connected by internal stone staircases. The timbers of two pivot-mounted wooden doors, each about six feet high, are evidence that the rooms were handsomely and securely closed off. The occupants used a great deal of pottery, some of exquisite design, incorporating reliefs of rams' heads, lions and ibexes.

This fragment of a 15th Century B.C. clay vase or incense burner records details of the actual walls of Hattusa. Windows in the tower permitted archers, shielded from enemy arrows, to shoot from several directions at once. The mud-brick crenelations had rounded rather than pointed edges, possibly to diminish erosion caused by the elements.

The house itself was a freestanding structure, and was laid out as if it had grown room by room; neither exterior nor interior walls ran in preplanned straight lines but instead were staggered and offset, producing a multiplicity of corners. Also, the ground on which the several levels of the building were constructed had been terraced.

This same basic architectural style had been well established in Anatolia before the Hittites arrived. The newcomers adopted it—even for temples and palaces built on a grand scale—as readily as they did the native gods and other local features that contributed to Hittite culture.

For several centuries under the Hattians the site grew in population until it became a true city. It is likely that most of the slope between the two original settlements was covered with houses. In time, a wall of mud brick on a stone foundation was thrown up to protect the summits, where the local princes probably resided, and it may have encompassed the lower community as well.

Situated near north-south and east-west trade routes, the city increased in commercial importance and at some point—probably during the 19th Century B.C.—attracted a *karum*, or colony, of Assyrian traders who occupied a suburb that they had built for themselves on the lower ground of the city's northern outskirts.

Then, late in the following century, came catastrophe: the entire city, including the Assyrian *karum*,

A modern archeological reconstruction shows some of the features of Hattusa in about the 13th Century B.C. The dashes (lower right) mark the line the Old City's walls are thought to have followed; the New City's walls have been located from surviving fragments of the original. The large building (1) in the Lower City is the Great Temple; structures 2 through 5 (upper left) represent other places of worship. On the citadel (center) was the royal residence. Nisantepe, Yenicekale and Sarikale may have been alternate royal residences.

burned to the ground. The devastation is believed to have been the work of Anitta, king of the Anatolian city of Kussara. Anitta, who was revered by later Hittite monarchs as the spiritual ancestor of them all, bragged at the time that he "sowed weeds" where Hattusa had stood. The site was abandoned and not rebuilt for a hundred years.

Its rebirth as a city came in the 17th Century B.C. when King Labarna II, who had already extended Hittite hegemony in Asia Minor and Syria, decided to build his capital on the ruins and take his name Hattusili from the site. Once again, the natural advantages of a plentiful water supply and defensible high ground were factors that weighed heavily in the decision to establish a capital there.

Later, in imperial times, when a hostile people called the Kaska had moved into the territory to the north, the Hittites would be grateful for Hattusa's location. The never-pacified Kaska warriors kept the empire's northern border continually in turmoil and threatened the capital for centuries. Even at the height of Hittite expansion, the boundary of effective Hittite control rarely extended more than a few dozen miles north of the city. Partly because of this and partly because of the vigorous and militant nature of the Hittites themselves, Hattusa became as much a fortress as a city. King Hantili, who reigned in the 16th Century B.C., surrounded it with protective walls, which, as the city expanded over the following centuries, were several times extended in order to embrace new additions.

In the 14th and 13th centuries B.C. Hattusa spread to its greatest size and achieved its greatest glory. The findings of archeologists and their interpretation by historians make it possible to visualize something of the magnificence of that imperial city at its zenith, and the hieroglyphic and cuneiform messages left by the Hittites help to shed light on the nature of its proud inhabitants. But archeology and the ancient writings can reveal only part of what Hattusa was like in that era. To recapture the flavor of the living city, it is necessary to relax the tight reins of scholarly discipline and make logical surmises, woven of the established random facts and of what is known about life in other Near Eastern cities that flourished around the same time.

A visitor to Hattusa during the 13th Century B.C. —say, a man from a vassal state who had never been to the capital before—probably would approach the city by its easiest access, across the relatively low land to the north. Although the countryside surrounding the ruins is now almost barren, his way may then have led through forests. At least one Hittite document suggests the fact. It describes a ritual during which the statue of a god was carried in a chariot, which was festooned with red, white and blue ribbons, through the northwestern gate to a brook, and then ceremonially bathed: "the women go in front, also the dancers and the temple harlots go in front, and they hold lighted torches," says the clay tablet, "and the god comes behind, and they take the god to the woods."

Coming out of the wooded area, the visitor would find himself standing in an open patch before the city —no military leader worth his salt would allow enemies the cover of trees close to his defenses. Here the visitor pauses to absorb the view. He has to lift his eyes, however, because the massive walls of Hattusa tower above the surrounding landscape—and the ground behind them rises sharply into a rocky fist clenched at the sky.

Having arrived at the first light of day, before the gates have been unlocked, the visitor decides that he will walk halfway around the circuit of walls. To go all the way around, he has been told, would entail a long and arduous hike, some four miles up and down slopes, over ridges, into gorges, across rushing streams. At one point in his stroll he is astonished to see the wall bridge a chasm 28 feet wide—no mean achievement of engineering. On the city's south side the walls are newer; they were constructed about the 14th Century B.C. in a flurry of urban expansion that doubled the enclosed area of Hattusa.

These fortifications, defending the Upper City, encompass the highest ground in the vicinity. In front of them a natural depression has been dug yet deeper by the Hittites, who used the excavated earth to increase the height of the rampart on which the walls were built. This rampart is paved with stones to form a glacis, a steep incline whose smooth surface denies foothold to any assaulting force.

Along the crest of the rampart runs the city's outer wall. A few yards behind it and towering above it is the main wall. Parapets with rounded crenelations run along the top, and at periodic intervals high towers with windows command views—and fields of fire—both to the front and to the sides.

While admiring the walls, the visitor has noticed that there are several entrances to the city—sally ports, pedestrian doors, and grand, tower-flanked gateways, at the tops of ramps, that can be negotiated by wagons or chariots. Here on the south side the outer wall is approached by two steep staircases angling up the rampart, both easily defended from the battlements above. Once through the outer fortifications, anyone entering the city has to pass along a ramp between the walls—not a pleasant gantlet for any would-be invader to run—in order to reach the gate in the main wall. The gate itself is flanked by carved stone sphinxes.

In peaceful times travelers to the city might be spared the long climb up the stairs. With the permission of a sentinel, travelers may go through a postern, or sally port—a tunnel more than 230 feet long that runs straight through the rampart, beneath the walls, emerging inside the city. While it can serve as a shortcut for a footsore pedestrian, this passage is primarily a defensive feature. Too narrow for enemies to use in order to enter the city in force, it provides an exit for Hittite soldiers slipping out for a sortie against besiegers.

Now, from inside the walls come voices and the clink of bolts. The gates are about to be opened. The visitor waits. According to regulations laid down by a king named Arnuwanda, who ruled around 1400 B.C., the city's security is the responsibility of the *hazannu*—a government official. "You, *Hazannu*, be very careful in matters of the guard, and in Hattusa the guard shall be well controlled," read Arnuwanda's instructions, inscribed on a clay tablet. "When they lift the copper bolts on the gate in the morning, when you have sent your son or servant to open the doors, when the seal on the gate turns, then afterward a man from Hatti or a commanding officer, or whoever is on duty, shall together examine the seal at the gate and open the gate accordingly."

The visitor hears the guards pull the copper bolts and wrestle the heavy crossbar from its niches cut into the stone. Then—with some grunting and the ap-

Text continued on page 123

Ingenious Defenses of the Imperial Capital

Even today, more than 3,000 years after Hattusa was reduced to ruin, remnants of its fortifications—like the massive gateway below—proclaim the Hittites' genius as military architects. Brilliantly taking advantage of the rugged terrain, the builders encircled their capital with a wall, in places 26 feet thick. In its nearly four-mile sweep, it traversed hills as well as low points that were filled in with earth to produce steep ramparts. It was based solidly on tiers of gigantic stones, many of them hewn into smooth blocks that fitted snugly without benefit of mortar. Atop these foundations, mud bricks were laid, and ponderous towers were erected to defend the city's many gates.

The Lion Gate, a major portal in the great wall that encircled Hattusa, was guarded by tall rectangular towers, whose block-built foundations jut out on either side. The gate, 10 feet wide at ground level, was named after the lions sculpted on its door jambs.

A Foolproof Security System

The main gates of Hattusa were by far the most dramatic feature of the city's extensive and varied defenses—calculated, doubtless, to reinforce the impression of the Hittites' might. One of the principal entrances to the city was the arched King's Gate *(below)*. Decorated with the figure of a muscular god carrying a battle-ax, it was flanked by twin stone towers. At night, the massive doors—made most probably of bronze-covered wood—were swung in place and copper bolts inserted. With the King's Gate and other gates thus locked and the city ringed securely by its thick walls on which soldiers kept the watch, the citizens of Hattusa could sleep the night through without fear of sudden attack.

The top-view diagram below reveals the complex construction of the King's Gate and its adjoining towers. The two double doors at center probably were closed from inside the gate chamber, after which the doorkeeper escaped by climbing a rope or ladder to the wall above. The six spaces inside each tower, formed by walls, were filled with rubble for added strength.

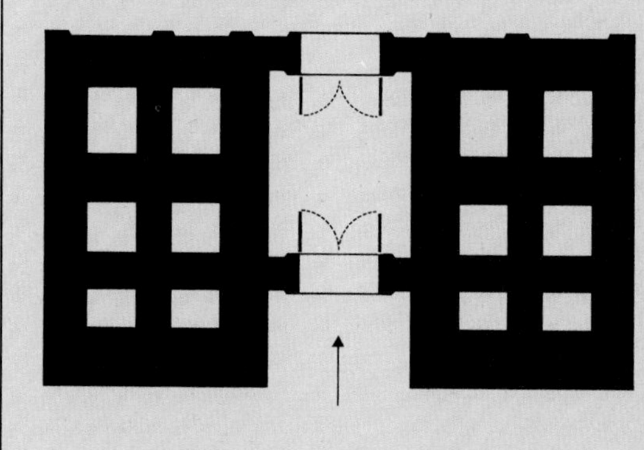

Carved on a door jamb, the powerful, regal figure of a god stands guard at the King's Gate.

The two reconstructions at right show features common to the King's Gate, the Lion Gate and Hattusa's two west gates. Each had two portals carved of stone in the shape of parabolic arches (far right). As seen in the cross section (near right), the watchtowers that flanked the gates were soundly built on deep underground foundations and were cut through by a walkway that ran around the top of the city wall.

The ruins of two arches, 26 feet apart and originally 15 feet high, suggest the colossal scale of the King's Gate and its flanking towers.

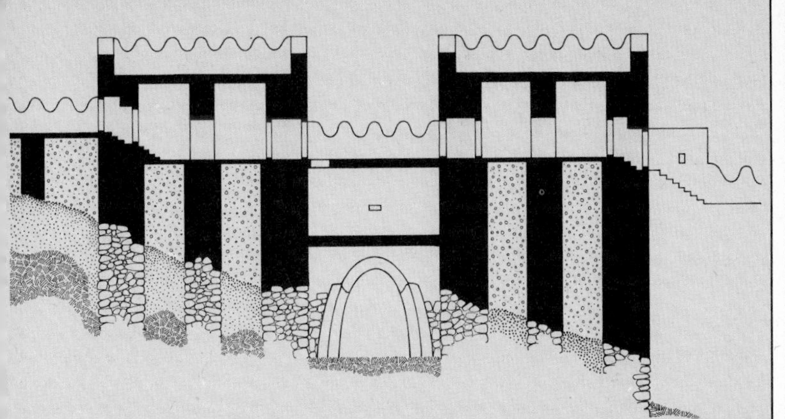

Vaulted Tunnels for Counterattack

To strengthen the defenses of Hattusa, Hittite engineers built nine stone posterns, or tunnels, with corbeled vaults, through which soldiers could dash out from beneath the city wall to attack a besieging army. These passageways were constructed at the capital's low or vulnerable sections, where dirt had been mounded up to make the defenses higher and steeper. The builders did not attempt to conceal their tunnels; the Earth Gate postern, illustrated on this page, terminated in plain view of the enemy. But its narrow exit could easily be defended by only a handful of soldiers.

Overlapping rows of stones form the long vault of the postern.

A simple doorway marks the tunnel's exit outside the capital.

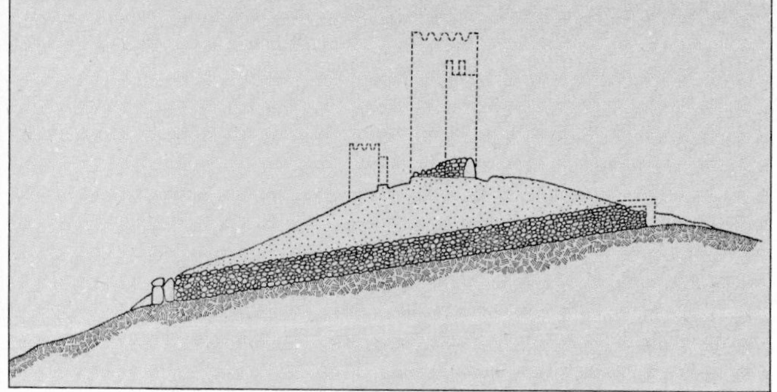

This schematized cross section of the 235-foot-long Earth Gate shows the general design of Hattusa's underground passageways. From its entrance inside the city, the tunnel slanted downhill, passing through the high dirt rampart underneath a tower in the city wall (center) to an exit beyond and below the fortifications.

plication of a shoulder or two—the big doors are heaved open. They are made of thick timber plated with bronze and are hung from huge wooden posts that pivot in holes carved in the rock of the sill below and the lintel above.

The way to Hattusa is now open and the visitor enters and passes through the dark, cool gate chamber where sentries stand in alcoves to either side. Having entered by a southern gate into the highest part of Hattusa, the visitor is surprised to find himself facing not a jumble of urban structures, but a big expanse of open ground, from which vantage point he can take in the panorama of the city. It is here that the people of outlying districts take refuge in times of strife. Nearby, close to the southeastern city wall, stand three large, flat-roofed buildings grouped together in a precinct surrounded by its own enclosure wall. Another structure of similar dimensions is just a little way down the hill. These four monumental edifices consist of stone and mud brick; even when seen at a distance, as from the lower end of the city, they are impressive. The visitor asks their purpose of a priest who is passing by; they are temples, the priest explains. Realizing that the visitor is a stranger, the priest offers to show him the city.

Beyond the four big temples Hattusa spills down the uneven slope of the mountainside for more than a mile. In the upper section, a number of large imposing houses—the homes of leading citizens—stand on their own individual terraces of raised earth. A half mile or so below them, to the east, a rising spur of ground is crowded with some even more imposing big buildings. They are ringed by still another fortified wall that eventually juts over a stream-gouged canyon. This is the royal complex, where the Great King lives with his family and his retainers and from which he rules the Hittite Empire.

Farther downhill, where the ground levels somewhat, is the Old City, built around the site of one of the two original hamlets from which Hattusa grew. There, flat-roofed houses jostle each other for standing room. One behemoth of a structure (actually a group of connected structures) is prominent among them. This is the Great Temple, the city's principal house of worship, devoted to the Storm God.

On the other side of the gorge, north of the royal palace, is the sharply rising prominence that makes such a striking sight when the city is viewed from the north. On its wall-enclosed crest rides a cluster of buildings. Beyond and below the wall at the far northern end of Hattusa lie the fields and woods through which the visitor came.

The Old City is already wide awake. The closely packed dwellings turn their backs on their neighbors and face private courtyards. Waste water gurgles from drain holes cut into the bottoms of the walls and sluices along the narrow alleyways that run between the houses. The aroma of smoking-hot olive oil coming from within tells the visitor that the occupants will soon be eating their morning meal.

Like all busy cities, Hattusa is a noisy place. Men dressed in simple tunics and bearing big earthen jugs pass by shouting jocular greetings to one another. The guide explains that these are slaves going to and from the city's springs to fetch water for the day. A small group of self-confident boys swings past, pushing and chattering and laughing among themselves. They are the sons of scribes on their way to the scribal school, which will qualify them to follow in their fathers' footsteps as part of the select minority of Hittites who can read and write.

At an intersection a gang of men with tools is being assembled by an official. He checks their names against a list and they answer without enthusiasm, grumbling among themselves. These are not slaves but freemen—town craftsmen and peasants from the nearby countryside called together to fulfill their obligation of *luzzi*, the forced labor periodically levied on all freemen as a kind of tax. They are going to spend the day working on the walls of Hattusa, which are regularly maintained.

There seems to be a lot of construction underway in the city, and it accounts for much of the noise. Up ahead, a team of carpenters sweats under the weight of a large wooden beam. They are trying to jockey it into place as a rafter for a half-finished house. As they maneuver, they call out several conflicting orders to each other and gesture their contempt for the directions given by one of their number who is perched on top of the wall.

The priest as self-appointed guide explains to the visitor that Hattusa is continually being rebuilt. Because of the winter snows and the spring rains, the roofs of mud and thatch require constant repair, and the houses made of unfired mud bricks rarely last 50 years, and often only 20.

Suddenly there come the clatter of horses' hooves, the rumble of wheels on paving stones and cries of warning. People quickly duck close to the walls on either side of the street. The Hittite guide quickly pushes the visitor into a doorway for safety just before the chariot rattles by.

The bronze-helmeted driver is a Hittite soldier, like those stationed at the city wall; his passenger is an older man whose dress and darker skin mark him as a foreigner. Is this a visiting dignitary, an ambassador perhaps, the visitor asks? The guide smiles and shakes his head. No, he replies. The Great King's daughter is ill. The chariot's passenger is an Egyptian physician who, by the generosity of his master, the pharaoh, has come all the way from Egypt to cure her. He is accompanied, moreover, by the statue of a powerful Egyptian god. There are rumors in Hattusa that a Babylonian doctor and magician are soon to arrive for the same purpose.

By importing foreign medical consultants, the Hittite king has acknowledged the backward state of Hittite medicine. Although there are some Babylonian medical texts to go by, local doctors are virtually shamans, who conduct their patients through rituals designed to cure them and who throw in a few therapeutic herbs for good measure.

The visitor and his companion walk on, passing doorways through which weavers, leatherworkers, potters and perhaps half a dozen other craftsmen can be seen working at their respective trades. One open doorway shows a room piled high with costly bolts of fine Assyrian cloth.

At the next intersection a small mixed herd of calves and lambs is being driven across the path, adding their lowing and bleating to the cacophony of city sounds. The herdsmen appear to be in a hurry, although one who recognizes the priest-guide offers him a quick smile and wave.

The visitor assumes they are on their way to the livestock exchange and asks where the market is located. Oh, no, he is told; the animals are being taken to a temple. They belong to the gods, and they must be delivered on time; written instructions for members of the priesthood (who, like the civil bureaucrats, want to have all the rules written down) are exacting about promptness. One clay tablet declares in no uncertain terms: "You who are the gods' shepherds, if there is a rite for any god . . . and you are supposed to have ready for him either a calf, a lamb, a kid or choice animals, do not delay them! Have them ready at the right time; do not let the gods wait for them." If undue delay should create suspicion that the herders have been purloining prime holy livestock for themselves and replacing it with inferior animals, it could mean death for the herders, their wives and children. No wonder they are in a rush.

Is today, then, a holy day? Yes, like so many other days here. A festival is to be celebrated at one of the temples. The visitor persuades his priest-friend to take him to it, and so they follow in the path of the men driving the livestock.

Having come some distance through the warren of the Old City, they now find themselves before the walls surrounding the Great Temple of the Storm God *(pages 126-127)*. They enter the temple enclosure through a portal that is almost as imposing as the gates in the city walls. On either side are sentries posted in their boxes within the colonnaded gatehouse. Once inside the portal, the priest and the visitor find themselves on a street that runs between a series of rooms built against the walls surrounding the temple and the rectangular temple proper at the center of the complex.

The guide suggests that he and the visitor first explore the rooms on the perimeter. A few yards from the gate they pass a great stone basin containing water. Judging from the number of people gathered around it, the basin serves as a public rendezvous point in addition to whatever ceremonial function it has. A musician plucks on a stringed instrument to check its tuning; another tootles idly on double pipes. Their clothes are bright and well tended. A man adjusts the angle of his close-fitting domed cap while a woman brushes an imagined mote of dust from her gown. Near the wall two young men glide and shuffle through a dance, watching their feet and counting out the steps aloud. The tingle of stage nerves is unmistakable; this is a troupe of entertainers awaiting its cue to perform at the festival.

The visitor and his guide move on. The street encircling the main temple structure is as busy as any in the city. Men carrying covered bowls and platters of food continually cross their path. Up ahead, the two strollers see the herdsmen they had earlier followed, driving the lambs and kids into one of the rooms against the outer wall. Other animals wander aimlessly; a pig pokes his head into an open doorway, provoking a chorus of shouts from within and winning himself a vigorous kick that sends him skittering on his way.

Here are the gods' kitchens, the guide explains to his friend, where standards of cleanliness are rigidly enforced. "You shall be bathed and dressed in clean garments," the regulations state emphatically. "Furthermore your body hair and your nails shall be removed. . . . If a pig or a dog somehow approaches the implement . . . and the kitchen's servant does not discard it, but gives the god to eat from an unclean vessel, to such a man the gods will give dung and urine to eat and drink."

Through an entrance the visitor and priest see bakers pulling freshly browned loaves from a clay oven. They slip in unnoticed and pass through an internal

The Colossal Temple of the Storm God

In Hattusa's Lower City, on a broad slope above the Anatolian plateau, the Hittites built an enormous temple complex. So elaborate was the plan, with its dozens of narrow storerooms, archival chambers and living quarters for priests and officials, that the Great Temple, begun in the 14th Century B.C., took decades of work to finish.

Completed during the mid-1200s, the complex was composed of two main buildings covering more than five acres—equivalent to the area taken up by five modern football fields. As the ground plan opposite shows, it was bisected by a wide street. Excavations indicate that the smaller section, to the south, probably served as the administrative center. The larger section consisted of four two- and three-storied wings surrounding the temple proper, with its inner courtyard and twin sanctuaries. The foundations were constructed of massive blocks of limestone, of which great sections *(left)* remain in place today.

The foundation stones of the temple complex form neat rectangles. The small holes in the blocks held wooden dowels that helped support the longitudinal beams. In the background may be seen clay storage vessels, still positioned where archeologists found them.

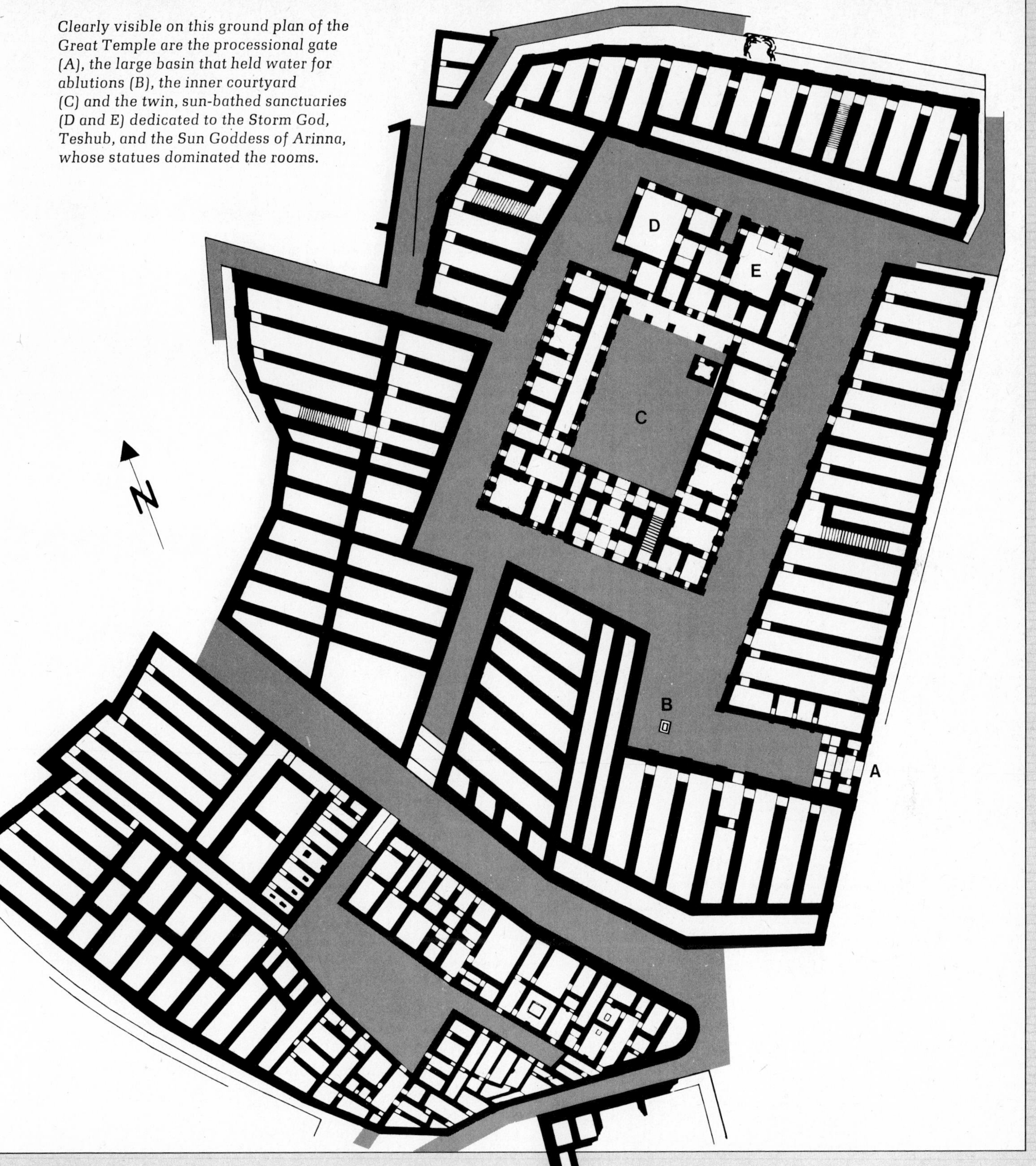

Clearly visible on this ground plan of the Great Temple are the processional gate (A), the large basin that held water for ablutions (B), the inner courtyard (C) and the twin, sun-bathed sanctuaries (D and E) dedicated to the Storm God, Teshub, and the Sun Goddess of Arinna, whose statues dominated the rooms.

doorway to the next room, where butchers are trimming fat from meat. They find that the rooms along the outer wall are almost all connected by interior doors, and they wander through them, finding more kitchens, storerooms for the gods' food and drink, and locked depositories of the gods' valuable possessions—costly and ornate robes, and implements of gold, silver, bronze and iron.

Safeguarding these treasures is a problem: the temple records spell out careful security measures. No priest is allowed to take away silver and gold (they are the property of the temple), and a priest becomes suspect if his wife or children wear ornaments made of precious metals. On occasion the king may give valuable personal gifts to priests. When this happens, a description of the item and its weight must be entered in the temple records, along with a note about when and where the gift was presented. Witnesses are required, for the records include such notations as "When they gave it to him, [so-and-so and so-and-so] were present."

Continuing their round, the visitor and his new friend find some of the rooms stacked high with clay tablets filed on wooden shelves, each lot indexed by a smaller tablet labeling the contents of that section. The guide tells him that this is the temple library; it not only contains transcripts of myths, rituals and temple rules but also includes many state documents. Since most treaties call on the gods to enforce the terms, what better place to keep such pacts than in a house of worship?

By now the visitor and priest have walked about a sixth of a mile along the rectangular path of the temple street and, their side excursion completed, are back where they started. Now they enter a gate that leads directly into the main temple structure. Here, too, there are alcoves for guards on both sides, in this case with windows looking out onto the street. They walk through and find themselves in a paved courtyard about 90 feet long and more than 60 feet wide. Three of the walls around it are on foundations of colossal limestone blocks that have been brought from a nearby quarry. The fourth side of the courtyard is a colonnade of stone pillars.

In a side room off the courtyard, a small group of priests is bent in study over something on a table: the warm entrails from a newly slaughtered animal. They are consulting the gods on a question of major importance. Divination is fundamental to Hittite religion, and like so much else in their faith, the Hittites adopted it from the Babylonians. To find out how the king should act on a matter of state—whether to make war on a neighboring people, for instance—the priests study birds in flight on a given day, or kill a lamb or a kid and examine its entrails, reading the answer in the conformation of the organs.

Skirting this interior room and another, the visitor and his guide approach the inner sanctum of the Storm God himself. As in all Hittite temples, the sanctuary may be entered only by the king and queen, their retinue and members of the temple staff. The guide explains that the walls here are of rare granite transported from distant quarries and that the treasure at the far end of the sanctuary is the golden idol of the Storm God.

From the sounds they hear it is apparent that several priests are in the sanctuary. The guide explains that some are heaping dishes with food and filling cups with wine to set before the idol. Others will approach the god with vessels of water and oil and begin to bathe and anoint his golden body. When done, they will reverently dress the statue again in a fine, flowing garment.

This is routine, the guide tells his visitor. Every day the Storm God's servants, the priests, minister to his needs as if he were a living, breathing being. Between the god's regular meals and the profusion of offerings left for him by a steady stream of devout worshipers—fruit, grain, bread, wine, cheese, olive oil, and lambs and calves whose throats are cut before him—his temple and sanctuary at times resemble a well-stocked food market.

There is a flourish of music from the courtyard, and the guide quickly ushers the visitor into a corner. The king is arriving to celebrate the festival. The music nears, and three men approach, one of them carrying a spear. He is a member of the king's bodyguard and his vigilant eyes take in the visitor and the guide but pass on, evidently judging them safe. Next a musician arrives, followed by dancers in yellow garments who spin wildly around and around, holding their hands high above their heads. And just behind them come the king and queen.

The royal couple, garbed in splendid robes, proceed at a stately pace. According to the guide, they will take their places on large thrones facing the god. Behind them more dancers twirl into the sanctuary, followed by the king's sons and a pride of Hittite nobles. A factotum seats the notables in the party according to rank, and then two priests bring the royal couple water in a vessel of gold. The king and queen wash their hands and dry them on a cloth provided by another priest.

A temple official, the verger, leaves the sanctuary and returns leading a parade of chief cooks bearing food covered with a cloth. Another official tells the king that entertainers outside await his pleasure. In a ceremonial voice, following established ritual, the king replies: "Let them come forth!" The man comes into the courtyard calling, "Music! Music!" Another voice further away, at the gate of the temple, picks up the cry. "Music! Music!"

Within a few moments the entertainers take up positions around the sanctuary. As they play, sing and dance, the cooks present the meal to the king, who removes the cloth and, again following established protocol, flings it through the air to kneeling servants. The festival has begun.

The ritual that follows lasts so long that the visitor wishes he, too, had a seat. A priest recites some long passages of religious text while sacrifices are offered to the Storm God. Finally, on a signal from an official, the company rises and the king and queen lead them from the sanctuary. The guide summons the visitor to follow the procession.

Along with the rest of the crowd of less privileged worshipers who pack the courtyard, they fall back respectfully to make a path for the royal party, which wends its way out of the temple precinct and through the city to one of the northern gates. The guide informs his visitor that the road beyond the gates leads out to a rock shrine, the walls of whose natural chambers are carved with figures of the gods. There the rites will continue.

The road crosses a rushing brook, climbs a steep embankment and then passes through an area cluttered with groups of stones marking the graves of important citizens. The procession has moved to a Hittite cemetery, where the ashes of once-important citizens—and in some cases their uncremated bodies—are buried, their coffins being large earthenware pots. Many common people, in contrast, are interred in the earth beneath their own homes.

The road ahead of them rises and the van of the procession disappears inside the flat-roofed temple buildings that form an entrance to the rock sanctuary. Instead of following, the guide then turns his visitor back toward the city.

Day is ending as they reenter Hattusa. The streets are quieter now. The carpenters are gone from the half-finished house, having fixed all its roof beams in position. Some of the work gang are returning from their day of required labor on the walls, looking tired but hurrying home with lighter spirits than they displayed at the start of the day.

In the dusk two priests, heads down and walking fast, brush past. They are returning to their temple, having been home to visit their families. "If the desire for a woman overcomes anyone," the priests' instructions declare, "let him sleep with a woman" but "promptly come up to spend the night in the temple." Perhaps they are among those scheduled for that night's guard duty. Each night, patrols under the command of a high priest keep watch both inside and outside the temple walls.

The city has its watchmen, too, overseen by the *hazannu*. Their chief concern is fire, the guide explains, which could spread rapidly in a town where heavily timbered houses crowd so close together. As darkness falls, the call of the first nightwatch floats over the rooftops: "Extinguish the fire!" Later, in the depths of the dark Anatolian night, the men who stand the middle nightwatch will call to sleeping Hattusa: "The fire shall be guarded!"

In this often savage world of the 13th Century B.C., a great city, confident in its fortifications and the efficiency of its organization, finds secure repose. The copper bolts hold fast the gates and the watchmen are on the walls. The citizens could not know that within the next hundred years the temples and palaces and homes of mighty Hattusa would be violently reduced to a smoking ruin of charred timbers and mud bricks reddened by fire.

An Illustrated Sampler of Hittite Myths

The world of Hittite myths was violent and mysterious, reflecting life in a powerful state whose leaders rose and fell and whose boundaries constantly shifted. Over the centuries innumerable gods in human form, often representing rivers, mountains and forces of nature, entered the pantheon as new peoples came under Hittite rule. Out of the resultant jumble, one consistent theme emerges, and that is struggle: dynasty against dynasty, good against evil, Everyman against the vicissitudes of fate.

Because the stories are so ancient, they frequently seem completely outside the present-day reader's frame of reference. Yet, as folk literature they share many qualities with the myths and fairy tales of later peoples; and thus, upon reflection, it is often possible to guess the meanings or morals. The three fables retold here have been pieced together from broken tablets unearthed from Hittite ruins and are illustrated in pen-and-ink drawings by a modern artist who took his inspiration from the Hittite style.

With dismay, the god Kumarbi considers the seeds he holds on his tongue, all of them embryonic deities. One will become Teshub, the all-important Storm God; another will take the form of the River Tigris; the third will become Tashmishu, a minion of the Storm God.

The Song of Ullikummi

The Song of Ullikummi has an unusual setting for a people who were basically oriented to the land. This myth takes place by the sea. It may have come into the literature of the Hittites by way of Syrian kingdoms that lay on the Mediterranean and that became Hittite vassals during the 14th Century B.C.

If the setting is odd, the motif was common enough: the constant challenges to supremacy that had to be met even by the most powerful. The ultimate victor of the particular contest illustrated here will have to be guessed, however, since the tablet breaks off at a crucial point in the story.

The Storm God, one of several deities born to Kumarbi *(preceding page)*, grew up to displace his father as king of the gods. Kumarbi sought revenge by siring another son, a monstrous creature formed of a kind of volanic rock called diorite. As Kumarbi dandled the new infant on his knee, he named him Ullikummi. "Let him ascend to heaven for kingship!" Kumarbi cried. "Let him attack the Storm God and chop him to pieces like straw! Let him tread him underfoot like an ant! Let him shoot down all the gods from the sky like birds and let him break them to pieces like empty pots!"

Kumarbi assigned care of the infant to a group of guardian deities. They took him down to the sea and perched him on the shoulder of Ubelluri, who the Hittites believed held heaven and earth aloft. And there the monstrous stone baby grew with magic swiftness. In a day he increased a cubit (roughly 18 inches), in 15 days he stood so tall that the sea "reached up to his belt like a loincloth."

The Storm God, the Sun God and all the other gods took fright at this alarming development, and after conferring among themselves, set out together to rout the monster. But they soon gave up in dismay. For Ullikummi kept right on growing, until he stood 9,000 leagues tall—so tall he "pushed up the sky like an empty garment." The gods conferred again and, on the advice of Ea, god of the subterranean waters, they fetched an ancient copper knife from the heavenly storehouse, and Ea used it to sever the monster's legs. That done, he told the gods, "I have crippled the diorite man. Go ye and battle him again!" While the rest of the gods merely began to "bellow like cattle against Ullikummi," the Storm God jumped into his chariot and went off to confront him. Here the tablet breaks off, just as Ullikummi roars that he will drive the Storm God and all the other deities from heaven.

Though the myth's ending is missing, it is assumed that the Storm God triumphs as the supreme deity, partly because he lives on in so many other myths, and partly because at the end of all folk tales everywhere an ugly or evil presence is usually eliminated one way or another.

Vying for supremacy among the gods in heaven, the Storm God raises a club against the monster Ullikummi, his half brother and rival for the throne. The Storm God's two sacred bulls, Sheri and Hurri, wait placidly below.

The Slaying of the Dragon

For all his eminence in the Hittite pantheon, the Storm God's rank among the gods was never entirely secure and he often had to fight to keep it. One of his challengers was the malevolent Illuyanka, a dragon —or, as the fearsome creature is also conceived in the myths, a serpent—and in several instances the Storm God needed mortal help to hold his own. In one version of this myth he begat a son to pit against the dragon *(page 103)*; in the version that is illustrated here he gave the task to his daughter Inara, who called on a man named Hupasiya to help her. Hupasiya agreed to do as she asked provided Inara would sleep with him, which she did.

Inara then set out a lavish banquet, with amphorae of wines and other beverages "filled to the brim." She put on her finery and went to the dragon. "See! I am holding a celebration," she said. "Come thou to eat and to drink." So the dragon climbed out of his hole in the ground, bringing with him all his children. They ate and drank until they had stuffed themselves, and while they nodded drowsily afterward, Hupasiya, who had been lurking unseen nearby, took the dragon unawares and bound him with a rope, whereupon the Storm God was able to slay him.

This story seems to belong to a category of myths found in many civilizations throughout the ages: the theme of the gluttonous and dull-witted villain being overcome by trickery. The Hittite dragon legend probably soothed the Hittites' human wish to believe that when all else failed—whatever the contest, whoever the foe and no matter how great the odds—a man would get by on his wits.

Once the menacing dragon was eliminated, Inara turned her attention to Hupasiya. She built a house on a cliff and installed him in it, ordering him never to look out the window. Then she departed, leaving him alone. Twenty days passed, and Hupasiya could not resist temptation; he dared look out the window. And down below he saw his wife and children. The sight made him homesick, and when Inara returned, he begged her to let him go home.

But he had disobeyed her orders, and she killed him. And the Storm God came and sowed weeds over the house where Inara had dwelt with Hupasiya. This phase of the tale concludes on a forlorn note: "That man," says the tablet, "came to a grievous end."

Did the Hittites take a moral from the second part of this story? Perhaps so. They doubtless felt that the human being who enters into affairs with the gods had best beware, and their experience with life had taught them that, in any case, little people seldom really count for much.

The Storm God, standing astride two mountain peaks and holding a club and the lightning bolts that are symbols of his office, contemplates revenge against a dragon that has defied his authority. To the right of him the goddess Inara holds a wine pitcher, and the unwary dragon (far right), followed by his evil progeny, slithers to the feast that will be his undoing. At the lower left the mortal Hupasiya waits in hiding, ready to bind the dragon with a rope.

alexander

The God Who Disappeared

One of the most charming Hittite myths is that of the vanishing god. It was told in various versions, involving several different divinities, but the most popular account centers on Telipinu, a son of the ubiquitous Storm God and a deity of many roles, among them god of agriculture and god of fertility.

The tale begins with Telipinu flying into a rage. What touched him off is a mystery, since the first 20 lines of the tablet on which this particular version appears are missing. In this circumstance, the story begins with a distracted Telipinu, made indignant for reasons unknown, putting his left shoe on his right foot and his right shoe on his left foot. He wanders off, and in his absence disaster overcomes the land. "Mist seized the windows, smoke seized the house," says the tablet. "In the fireplace, the logs were stifled, at the altars the gods were stifled, in the fold the sheep were stifled, in the stable the cattle were stifled."

As misfortune piles upon misfortune, the other gods lament Telipinu's departure, and one after another they go in quest of him. One after another they fail to find him. At the behest of the Sun God, an eagle searches "every high mountain, the deep valleys and the watery depth," but it has no luck either. At last, the mother of the gods dispatches a bee to take up the search—a proposal that causes the Storm God to scoff: "The great gods and the lesser gods have searched for him but did not find him. Shall then this bee go out and find him? Its wings are small, it is small itself."

But the bee succeeds where all the others failed. It finds Telipinu asleep in a distant meadow—and, to awaken him, stings his hands and feet. Telipinu leaps up—shocked into a further spasm of anger. "How

dare you arouse me from my sleep?" he thunders. And he sends further plague upon the land: "He stopped the murmuring springs, he diverted the flowing rivers and made them flow over their banks. He shattered the windows, he shattered the houses."

The goddess of magic and healing, Kamrusepa, rushes to Telipinu and attempts to lure him back. She proffers him essence of cedar, figs, ointment, malt, honey and cream, and other delicacies: "Just as honey is sweet, as cream is smooth, even so let Telipinu's soul become sweet and even so let him become smooth." Finally she implores: "O Telipinu, give up thy rage, give up thine anger, give up thy fury!"

At long last Telipinu is soothed and is persuaded to return home—and all is well once more: "The mother tended her child, the ewe tended her lamb, the cow tended her calf. And Telipinu tended the king and the queen, and provided them with enduring life and vigor."

The myth suggests the bleakness of winter and the general rebirth that comes with spring everywhere. But the metaphor addresses itself as well to the vicissitudes of fortune—and indicates that where the high and mighty fail, less conspicuous folk can sometimes succeed. The Hittites recited the narrative when calamity made it appear that their gods had left them in the lurch, and accompanied their recitation with symbolic offerings similar to those with which the goddess Kamrusepa tempted Telipinu.

With his shoes on the wrong feet (far left, above), the god Telipinu goes off in a huff, leaving the land to perish. Later mollified through the efforts of a bee, an eagle and a goddess, he returns home (right) and the land recovers.

Chapter Seven: An Abrupt, Mysterious End

The empire's death was swift, catastrophic and—to historians of today—inexplicable. At some point, around 1200 B.C., scribes in Hattusa ceased writing records. What little is known about the Hittites after that date is either culled from the texts of outsiders or based on scholarly conjecture.

Ironically, the king who witnessed the end of the empire bore the same name as the mighty monarch who built it: Suppiluliuma. But the rule of this second Suppiluliuma, who ascended to the throne around 1215 B.C., must have been brief. The texts surviving from his reign are limited, and they provide few real clues to the reason for the empire's demise.

That Great Hatti's collapse was as violent as it was final is strikingly apparent to archeologists who have excavated Hattusa: the city was ravaged. Fire, the dreaded enemy against which the city's watchmen had guarded for centuries, razed its buildings to the ground. A layer of burned debris bears witness to a conflagration. The inner sides of the city's walls still show the marks of flame. Wherever sun-dried mud bricks had been used, hard red shards remain: intense heat converted Hattusa into a giant kiln, turning its building blocks to ceramic. Even on the heights of the citadel, nothing more than the foundations of the royal palace survived.

What the charred ruins make tragically plain is that a force—or forces—of furious antagonists smashed and torched their way through the city with stunning violence. So intense was their desire to erase or demolish all signs of the Hittite presence that they hammered stone sculptures to pieces. In one stroke, Hattusa was transformed from a proud metropolis to a lifeless specter that still haunts the historians and excavators of today.

Whoever the invaders were, they seem to have appeared all over the empire at once, laying waste other urban centers, driving the Hittites and their surviving subjects into desperate exile, utterly rending the imperial fabric that had once bound them together. Great Hatti was dead.

But who were its executioners? Scholars have suggested numerous candidates but, lacking conclusive evidence, agree on none. The Hittites may have destroyed themselves. Some of their last texts hint at dissension and rebellion within the empire. "The inhabitants of Hatti sinned against His Majesty," noted a scribe in the time of Suppiluliuma II. "His Majesty, my Lord, found the inhabitants of Hatti to be in revolt," recorded another. But beyond these sparse references, there is no proof of actual revolution. Anyway, internal turmoil—however much it may have weakened the Hittites' ability to resist invasion—could hardly account for the dispersal of the once great Hittite people and the dismantling of the empire. It is more likely that foreigners, rather than Hittite dissenters, were responsible for the downfall of Hatti—but who could they have been?

Powerful neighbors, most of them one-time enemies, had been exerting pressure on the empire well before 1200 B.C. In the southeast, in about 1242 B.C., King Tukulti-Ninurta of Assyria had cockily tested the border and boasted of carrying away 28,800 Hittite subjects. In response, the Hittites set up trade em-

Its mouth wide open in a roar, a stone lion stands guard over the ruins of Hattusa. One of a pair, it escaped the damage inflicted on its mate during fighting that completely destroyed the city and saw the demise of the Hittite Empire and the dispersal of its people around 1200 B.C. Who the vanquishers were is one of the most persistent enigmas of Hittite history.

Vestiges of a Vanished Culture

With the abrupt demise of the empire, around 1200 B.C., the Hittites themselves disappeared from record for so long that archeologists today hesitate to consider as true descendants the people who cropped up a couple of centuries later along the southeastern periphery of the old domain.

Nevertheless, they are called Hittites in the Bible, and they used Hittite hieroglyphs on many of their stone monuments. They also adopted some Hittite gods as their own, and their sculptors, for the most part, worked in a somewhat modified Hittite style. But the subjects of their art often differed greatly from those of their predecessors, typically—as in the reliefs at right—in the mundane nature of the scenes portrayed.

Their hair worn neo-Hittite style, the children of an Eighth Century B.C. king play games.

Still another storm god, circa 1000 B.C., with familiar conical hat and turned-up boots, receives a libation from a neo-Hittite ruler.

A tombstone memorializes a devoted married couple. The man, holding grapes, may have been a vintner.

bargoes against Assyria, whose merchants had done business in Anatolia on and off since 1900 B.C.

To the north, the Kaskan people were still demonstrating their irrepressible enmity for the Hittites. Though not an organized nation, the belligerent Kaskan tribesmen had been a thorn in Hatti's northern flank for at least 150 years. Sometime around 1300 B.C., when the Hittites' energies were absorbed elsewhere, the Kaska even managed to penetrate Hattusa's defenses and plunder the city. The Hittites eventually regained control of the place, but scholars generally agree that the Kaska must have played a role in the empire's undoing—if only by keeping the Hittites so distracted that they could not give their full attention to other pressing matters.

Somewhere to the west, there may have been trouble as well with the kingdom of Ahhiyawa—a country frequently mentioned in the Hittite royal records, but one that historians have failed to identify or locate on a map. The more daring theorists equate Ahhiyawa with Greece, the land of the Achaeans of Homeric legend who ruled the Greek mainland peninsula. (The names Ahhiyawa and Achaea do indeed suggest similarities.) Other experts speculate that Ahhiyawa was one of the Mediterranean island kingdoms—on Crete, Rhodes or Cyprus. A more conservative view is that Ahhiyawa was a neighbor of Hatti's, situated on the coast of Anatolia, far to the west of the Hittite capital.

Wherever it was that the Ahhiyawans lived, they seem at first to have been treated by the Hittites with some friendliness. Correspondence records the fact that members of the Ahhiyawan royal family journeyed to Hattusa to master the charioteers' art, and also that when the Hittite king Mursili II lay ill, his priests and physicians imported a statue of an Ahhiyawan god to help cure him.

But at some point this cordial rapport deteriorated into antagonism for reasons that are still obscure. In one surviving text, a Hittite king had his scribe list "the kings who are of equal rank to me: the king of Egypt, the king of Babylon, the king of Assyria and the king of Ahhiyawa." But subsequently he seems to have ordered the last-named monarch to be struck from the roster; although an obvious effort was made to rub out the words, they can still be distinguished. Perhaps the erasure was motivated by a growing spirit of ill will, since other texts indicate that the Ahhiyawans, seeking to extend their own territory, had begun to interfere with Hatti's western dominions; late in the 13th Century B.C. the Ahhiyawans were supporting rebellion in Hittite vassal states.

An even bigger threat to Hittite stability came in the form of aggressive seafarers who appeared in the eastern Mediterranean in the 13th and 12th centuries B.C. They represented a mixed bag of peoples, including Tyrrhenians, possibly Ahhiyawans, probably several groups from the coast of Asia Minor; some may even have come from as far away as Sicily and Sardinia. One band, the Philistines, eventually settled in the land that was to be named for them: Palestine. These various invaders are referred to collectively as the Sea Peoples.

The Sea Peoples were piratical. They ravaged the coast of Syria and attacked Ugarit, one of Hatti's rebellious maritime vassal states. Sometime late in the 13th Century B.C. the frantic king of Ugarit, seeking military aid, dispatched an urgent letter to a neighboring monarch. "Behold, the enemy's ships came here; my cities were burned and they did evil things in my country. Do you not know that all my troops and chariots are in the Hittite country, and all my ships in the land of Lycia? . . . Thus the country is abandoned to itself—the seven ships of the enemy that came here inflicted much damage upon us."

Apparently awed as little by the Egyptians as by any other adversaries, the Sea Peoples more than once took on the mighty fleets of Egypt itself. In the record of his reign that Pharaoh Ramses III ordered to be carved on the walls of his temple at Medinet Habu, there is a hint of what happened to the Hittites: "The foreign countries plotted in their island homelands . . . and no land could stand before their arms, beginning with Hatti, Kode, Carchemish, Arzawa and Alasiya. They came . . . onward to Egypt."

But it is just a tantalizing inkling; no record survives to confirm that the Sea Peoples did indeed vanquish the Hittites. And Egyptian records are not altogether trustworthy in telling the whole truth about Egypt's old rival. Although the Sea Peoples certainly combined land movements with their naval assaults, some historians cannot accept the idea that an enemy whose power was principally maritime could penetrate so deep into the heart of Anatolia.

If not the Sea Peoples alone, then some combination of foes—Hittite rebels, Assyrians, the Kaska, Ahhiyawans and others, too—may have participated in the demolition of the empire. Certainly, none of the Hittites' rivals would have lamented the news that Great Hatti was no more.

The empire's demise came at a time of mass migrations. It was one of those recurring periods when whole populations pulled up their tent pegs and moved to new camping grounds, often forcing the previous occupants to do the same. Thus, the Hittites —or what remained of them—went elsewhere. Just where is yet another of the mysteries. It has even been suggested that some went to Italy and eventually established the Etruscan culture. The Hittites' departure from Anatolia was reminiscent of their arrival there some 700 years before, when some unknown force compelled them to emigrate from the northern lands they had previously occupied. Whoever moved into central Anatolia in their wake apparently represented a less advanced degree of civilization, and the Hittite homeland plunged into a dark age, about which little is conclusively known.

Historians cannot be certain about who was first to resettle the place or exactly when. They are commonly held to have been Phrygians, whose home had been on the west coast of the Black Sea. Whoever they were, they built directly on top of the ruins of Hattusa; archeologists have found no layer of sediment to indicate the passage of a long time between occupying peoples.

Although the new residents instinctively homed in on the prominence known as the citadel, their settlement was in sharp contrast to the proud palace that once had stood there. They lived among the fallen walls without attempting to reconstruct them, using the rubble as building material for crude one-room houses, which were jumbled about the site without noticeable planning.

In some unexplained way, however, they must have had an understanding of the dead capital's shattered features. Amid the tumbled stones of the Lower City's huge temple, the squatters built a small shrine for their own worship. It had benches along the walls, an offering basin and a pedestal that may have held an idol. Perhaps the atmosphere of reverence was heightened by the monumental ruins that dwarfed the new little sanctuary.

Though after 1200 B.C. the great empire was no more, a ghost of Hittite civilization lingered for another 500 years in Syria and in southeastern Anatolia. The pale specter took the form of some 15 petty kingdoms whose inhabitants were called Hittites by their neighbors. But these successors most likely were not Hittites—at least not direct descendants. The peoples of these disparate states are known today as the neo-Hittites; they are an enigma in their own right.

When historians first began to unravel the strands that led to the story of the empire, some presumed the neo-Hittites to be the direct descendants of the empire builders, that invaders had driven them to seek refuge in former Hittite provinces in Syria and southeastern Anatolia. Other scholars ventured that the neo-Hittites traced back to the inhabitants of one-time subject nations. In fact, there probably were traces of both strains among them. They perpetuated certain cultural elements that were indisputably Hittite. At the same time, however, they had many traits that bore no relation at all to Hittite tradition.

The language of some neo-Hittites was a dialect of Luwian, which had been used in some parts of the empire. Others spoke Aramaic, a Semitic language unrelated to the Indo-European tongue. Most neo-Hittite cities had names that differed completely from any used in the age of empire. And except for provincial gods, none of the major deities survived in the neo-Hittite pantheon.

On the other hand, some neo-Hittite kings had names that clearly echoed the glorious monarchs of the past: Lubarna (Labarna), Sapalulme (Suppiluliuma), Katuzuli (Hattusili) and Mutallu (Muwatalli). The neo-Hitties inherited—or perhaps just adopted—the same hieroglyphic script found at Hattusa. Curiously, though, they seem not to have used the Hittites' more practical cuneiform writing.

The substance of the neo-Hittite hieroglyphic inscriptions sheds little light on who they were and what they did. Most of these texts were formal dedications, not revealing narratives. Clearly the neo-Hittites did not inherit their namesakes' fascination with self-chronicling. Their art, rather than their inscriptions, furnishes a glimpse of their personality.

On the whole, they seem to have been an affluent and contented people. Unlike Hittite stone carvers of the imperial era, their artists concentrated more on everyday life and its pleasures *(pages 140-141)* than on religion and statecraft. Musicians, children and animals were common subjects. A formal portrait of the Carchemish royal family shows the queen holding a baby and tugging by a leash a pet of indeterminate species, possibly a goat (neo-Hittite artistic standards were not very high). When chariots were involved, the scene was as likely to be an exhilarating hunt as a battle.

In a carving found among the neo-Hittite ruins at Karatepe, boisterous diners are seen lifting their cups high and digging into a sumptuous banquet while musicians play and a column of waiters hurries in with more food. Other servants pull and push a reluctant calf—not necessarily on his way to a ritual sacrifice, but perhaps to no more spiritual a destiny than to be the next course on the menu.

Such mundane scenes support the probability that these easygoing people lacked the sterner stuff of

Standing on the shore of an algae-choked pond in southern Anatolia, this weather-eroded structure of sculpted blocks remains an enigma to Hittitologists. No one knows what function it served. One scholar suggests that it was built during the last years of the Hittite Empire as a shrine to the Sun God, represented by the winged sun disks running horizontally across its broad façade.

their imperial namesakes—and this lack, it seems, was their undoing. By the Eighth Century B.C., Assyria—an old wolf feeling renewed vigor—was ready to descend on the fold, and the neo-Hittites were the sheep. The Assyrians had set about reconquering their old possessions east of the Euphrates, and eventually they expanded their conquests west of the river into land that Hittite kings had prevented them from entering. Solidarity among the neo-Hittite city-states might have stopped them, but instead each paid tribute to the Assyrians, who continued their triumphal march across Syria to the sea. In time the neo-Hittites paid for their acquiescence; one by one, the neo-Hittite kingdoms of Syria were absorbed into the Assyrian Empire; gradually their old languages and cultures faded completely. By around 700 B.C., even the Hittite ghost was dead.

So the Hittites came, conquered, ruled and vanished. By the Fifth Century B.C., when the Greeks traveled through the lands that had been the Hittite Empire, the name of Hatti was already forgotten.

What clear contributions, if any, did the Hittites bequeath to the progress of later civilizations? Many scholars—including that special breed, the Hittitologists—would tend to say few, or even none at all. It is true that none of the Hittites' influential successors—the Assyrians, the Hebrews, the Greeks—would have claimed, "We trace this tradition or that heritage to the Hittites." Yet modern scholars have found that there is indeed an inheritance—of a kind.

Professor Harry A. Hoffner, Jr. of the Oriental Institute at the University of Chicago, for example, sees some striking similarities between religious practices reflected in the Old Testament and the beliefs and prayers of the Hittites. According to Samuel I, one way a mortal could make contact with the gods of the underworld or with his ancestors (though the method was frowned upon by the Israelites) was through a hole dug into the ground. The Hittites also sought to communicate with infernal spirits in this way. There are, too, in the language of the Bible close parallels to Hittite texts—for instance, in a familiar passage from Isaiah: "In the desert prepare the road of Yahweh! . . . Make a straight highway for our God! Every valley shall be elevated; every mountain and hill shall be brought low. The crooked shall become straight, and the rough places a plain." The words echo a Hittite incantation to welcome a goddess called Wisuriyanza: "Eat, you awesome deity! Before you let the rivers be bridged! Before you let the valleys be leveled! Let the mountains betake themselves down to the vegetation!"

Professor Hans G. Güterbock, also of the University of Chicago, has drawn parallels between the mythologies of the Classical Greeks and the Hittites. The epic fights between the Greek gods Uranus, Cronus and Zeus for the monarchy of heaven, says Güterbock, has a likely Hittite antecedent. The Hittite story, adapted from a Hurrian tale, recounts how kingship of the gods passed in a series of battles to the Storm God, Teshub; Teshub corresponds to the Greek god Zeus. From the same cycle of Hittite myths, the god Ubelluri, who carried on his shoulder the land, the seas and the heavens, was quite possibly an ancestor of Atlas.

Just how such Hittite vestiges made their way into Greek lore some 500 years later is a question yet to be resolved. Possibly they were passed on secondhand, having been kept alive in Syrian culture until the Greeks came through that territory and salvaged them. Or they may have been transported, along with other aspects of their culture, by Hittites living among Greek-speaking peoples after the debacle.

Furthermore, the Hittite legacy, though most of it is intangible, includes two types of documents that influenced not only later cultures of the Near East, but also the modern world. The first is the treaty—the written agreement that bound lesser states to the empire. The Hittites may not have invented such pacts, but certainly they developed the treaty concept to a more complex level than had any people before them, and they made wider and more varied use of it than had any of their predecessors.

The second type of document is what scholars call royal annals—the narrative, year-by-year chronicle of the outstanding events of a king's reign. It had long been established that other, later Near Eastern peoples, principally the Assyrians, kept such records. But with the rediscovery of the Hittites came the realization that they possibly were the earliest people to write their own history in annal form. By the 17th Century B.C., during Hattusili I's reign, the keeping of royal annals had already begun. King Mursili II, who ruled in the 14th Century B.C., further refined the art; not only did he chronicle his own exploits in both an abbreviated and a detailed record, but he also commissioned the writing of the military deeds of his father, King Suppiluliuma I. With the faithful keeping of such annals, the Hittites gave 20th Century scholars the opportunity to see them as they really were—not merely as the butt of Egyptian slanders or as bit players in the Bible, but as a mighty, proud and resourceful people who built and administered one of history's first and greatest empires.

The Changing Forms and Moods of Hittite Gods

Like many other empire builders, the Hittites elevated their civilization on cultural borrowings from conquered or neighboring peoples. This pattern can be detected in every phase of Hittite life. But it shows up with special clarity in the Hittites' handsome representations of their gods.

Many of these deities, as well as the styles of portraying them, were adopted from the Hattians and other peoples who inhabited the Anatolian region of Turkey when the migrating Hittites made it their home in the 20th Century B.C. The gods also show the outside influences of Mesopotamia and, later, Egypt. It was not until the 14th Century, when the Hittite Empire reached its peak, that these varied borrowings were fused into a style that was distinctively Hittite.

During the intervening centuries, the gods changed dramatically in scale and mood. In early Hittite art, most idols were exquisite, passive, semi-abstract figures no more than a few inches high. But the gods grew apace with Hittite conquests, and the typical deity of the imperial age emerged as a vigorous, confident, realistic figure, standing several feet tall.

Twin gods, carved in limestone before 2000 B.C., show a pre-Hittite form of the double-image motif that Hittite artists later adopted as their own (page 17). This idol, measuring seven inches high, was probably used in fertility rites.

Cut from sheet gold, the pre-Hittite idol above is another example of the twin-god sculpture shown on the previous page. Its small size—just over one inch high—indicates that it was intended for personal use, and its place of discovery, a grave in the metalworking center of Alaça Hüyük, suggests it was made by a local smith between 2300 and 2100 B.C.

Rough in texture but refined in its Hattian craftsmanship, the four-inch-tall goddess at left was made of silver, with blue dots for eyes and gold inlays for ears, shoes and breasts. Since she is cupping her breasts, experts assume that she represents the goddess of fertility, who was often portrayed similarly elsewhere in the Near East.

A stylized goddess (right), one of the great masterpieces of Hattian art, is made of silver, with a gold-plated head (enlarged photograph). Only nine inches tall, the statuette may have been modeled after a Hattian princess who died around 2000 B.C.; her peaceful, solemn face and her slender, folded arms express a feeling of deep piety.

A Hittite god (above), carved in rock crystal between 1500 and 1200 B.C., has the broad face and stocky physique of the Hittites themselves. Though less than three inches high, it projects a sense of monumentality akin to that of much larger statues of the period.

An inch-high ivory figurine (left), the painstaking work of a Hittite artist who lived in the 14th Century B.C., can be identified as a god by its conical crown, and specifically as a mountain god by its tiered and sectioned skirt.

A striding god, made of gold in the 14th Century B.C., demonstrates the Hittites' growing interest in—and talent for—depicting action realistically. The tiny god (less than two inches tall) carries what seems to be a mace or staff. The ring on his back may have been a loop used to hang the figurine from a chain worn around the neck.

Apparently inspired by the Egyptian sphinx, this beast —an oversized lion with wings and human head (above and right)—nevertheless exemplifies the growing originality of Hittite artists during the great age of empire. In striking contrast to the impassive, conventionalized Egyptian creature, the 14th Century Hittite sphinx conveys a sense of individuality and animation. The goddess' face, which may represent the Hittite ideal of feminine beauty, is enlivened by a subtle smile and eyes that seem alert and expressive even though the inlay that once filled them is missing.

A muscular god (left), advancing purposefully in warrior's attire, reflects the power, ambition and confidence of the Hittites in their imperial age. As conquests enlarged the empire, small idols made for personal use were supplanted in artistic importance by grandiose figures carved for public display. This god stands six feet six inches tall and, like the sphinx at right, guarded a monumental stone gate at Hattusa (pages 120-121).

The Emergence of Man

This chart records the progression of life on earth from its first appearance in the warm waters of the new-formed planet through the evolution of man himself; it traces his physical, social, technological and intellectual development to the Christian era. To place these advances in commonly used chronological sequences, the column at the

Geology	Archeology	Billions of Years Ago	
Precambrian earliest era		4.5	Creation of the Earth
		4	Formation of the primordial sea
			First life, single-celled algae and bacteria, appears in water
		3	
		2	
		1	
		Millions of Years Ago	
			First oxygen-breathing animals appear
		800	
			Primitive organisms develop interdependent specialized cells
Paleozoic ancient life		600	Shell-bearing multicelled invertebrate animals appear
			Evolution of armored fish, first animals to possess backbones
		400	Small amphibians venture onto land
			Reptiles and insects arise
			Thecodont, ancestor of dinosaurs, arises
Mesozoic middle life			Age of dinosaurs begins
		200	Birds appear
			Mammals live in shadow of dinosaurs
			Age of dinosaurs ends
		80	
Cenozoic recent life			Prosimians, earliest primates, develop in trees
		60	
		40	Monkeys and apes evolve
		20	
		10	Ramapithecus, oldest known primate with apparently manlike traits, evolves in India and Africa
		8	
		6	
		4	Australopithecus, closest primate ancestor to man, appears in Africa

Geology	Archeology	Millions of Years Ago	
Lower Pleistocene oldest period of most recent epoch	Lower Paleolithic oldest period of Old Stone Age	2	Oldest known tool fashioned by man in Africa
		1	First true man, Homo erectus, emerges in East Indies and Africa
			Homo erectus populates temperate zones
		Thousands of Years Ago	
Middle Pleistocene middle period of most recent epoch		800	Man learns to control and use fire
		600	
			Large-scale, organized elephant hunts staged in Europe
		400	Man begins to make artificial shelters from branches
		200	
Upper Pleistocene latest period of most recent epoch	Middle Paleolithic middle period of Old Stone Age		Neanderthal man emerges in Europe
		80	
Last Ice Age		60	Ritual burials in Europe and Near East suggest belief in afterlife
			Woolly mammoths hunted by Neanderthals in northern Europe
		40	Cave bear becomes focus of cult in Europe
	Upper Paleolithic latest period of Old Stone Age		Cro-Magnon man arises in Europe
			Asian hunters cross Bering Land Bridge to populate New World
			Oldest known written record, lunar notations on bone, made in Europe
			Man reaches Australia
			First artists decorate walls and ceilings of caves in France and Spain
		30	Figurines sculpted for nature worship
		20	Invention of needle makes sewing possible
			Bison hunting begins on Great Plains of North America
Holocene present epoch	Mesolithic Middle Stone Age	10	Bow and arrow invented in Europe
			Pottery first made in Japan

Four billion years ago

Three billion years ago

Origin of the Earth (4.5 billion)

First life (3.5 billion)

far left of each of the chart's four sections identifies the great geological eras into which the earth's history is divided by scientists, while the second column lists the archeological ages of human history. The key dates in the rise of life and of man's outstanding accomplishments appear in the third column (years and events mentioned in this volume of The Emergence of Man appear in bold type). The chart is not to scale; the reason is made clear by the bar below, which represents in linear scale the 4.5 billion years spanned by the chart—on the scaled bar, the portion relating to the total period of known human existence *(far right)* is too small to be distinguished.

Geology	Archeology	Years B.C.	
Holocene *(cont.)*	**Neolithic** New Stone Age	9000	
			Sheep domesticated in Near East
			Dog domesticated in North America
		8000	Jericho, oldest known city, settled
			Goat domesticated in Persia
			Man cultivates his first crops, wheat and barley, in Near East
		7000	Pattern of village life grows in Near East
			Catal Hüyük, in what is now Turkey, becomes largest Neolithic city
			Loom invented in Near East
			Cattle domesticated in Near East
		6000	Agriculture begins to replace hunting in Europe
			Copper used in trade in Mediterranean area
	Copper Age		Corn cultivated in Mexico
		4800	Oldest known massive stone monument built in Brittany
		4000	Sail-propelled boats used in Egypt
			First city-states develop in Sumer
			Cylinder seals begin to be used as marks of identification in Near East
		3500	First potatoes grown in South America
			Wheel originates in Sumer
			Man begins to cultivate rice in Far East
			Silk moth domesticated in China
			Horse domesticated in south Russia
			Egyptian merchant trading ships start to ply the Mediterranean
			Pictographic writing invented in Near East
	Bronze Age	3000	Bronze first used to make tools in Near East
			City life spreads to Nile Valley
			Plow is developed in Near East
			Accurate calendar based on stellar observation devised in Egypt
		2800	Stonehenge, most famous of ancient stone monuments, begun in England
			Pyramids built in Egypt
			Minoan navigators begin to venture into seas beyond the Mediterranean

Geology	Archeology	Years B.C.	
Holocene *(cont.)*	**Bronze Age** *(cont.)*	2600	Variety of gods and heroes glorified in *Gilgamesh* and other epics in Near East
		2500	Cities rise in the Indus Valley
			Earliest evidence of use of skis in Scandinavia
			Earliest written code of laws drawn up in Sumer
			Use of bronze in Europe
		2000	Chicken and elephant domesticated in Indus Valley
			Eskimo culture begins in Bering Strait area
		1500	Invention of ocean-going outrigger canoes enables man to reach islands of South Pacific
			Ceremonial bronze sculptures created in China
			Imperial government, ruling distant provinces, established by Hittites
		1400	Iron in use in Near East
			First complete alphabet devised in script of the Ugarit people in Syria
			Hebrews introduce concept of monotheism
	Iron Age	1000	Reindeer domesticated in Eurasia
			Phoenicians spread alphabet
		900	
		800	Use of iron begins to spread throughout Europe
			First highway system built in Assyria
			Homer composes *Iliad* and *Odyssey*
			Mounted nomads appear in the Near East as a new and powerful force
		700	Rome founded
			Wheel barrow invented in China
		200	Epics about India's gods and heroes, the *Mahabharata* and *Ramayana*, written
			Water wheel invented in Near East
		0	Christian era begins

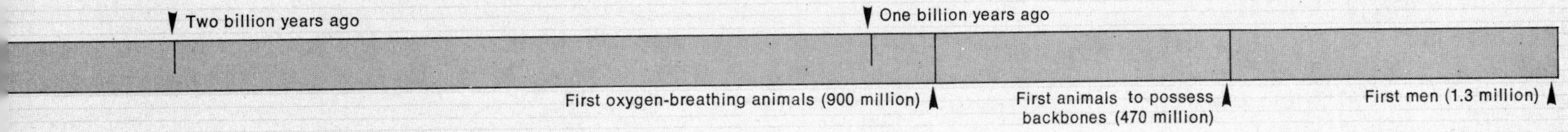

Two billion years ago

One billion years ago

First oxygen-breathing animals (900 million)

First animals to possess backbones (470 million)

First men (1.3 million)

Credits

The sources for the illustrations in this book are shown below. Credits from left to right are separated by semicolons, from top to bottom by dashes.

Cover—Painting by Michael A. Hampshire. 8—Fulvio Roiter. 11—Ozan Sagdic courtesy Ankara Archaeological Museum. 13—Maps by Rafael D. Palacios. 15—Photo Maurice Chuzeville, Musée du Louvre, Paris—Courtesy of the Oriental Institute, University of Chicago. 16—Hirmer Fotoarchiv, Munich courtesy Ankara Archaeological Museum. 17—Hirmer Fotoarchiv, Munich courtesy Ankara Archaeological Museum; Hirmer Fotoarchiv, Munich courtesy Alaça Hüyük Museum. 18, 19, 22, 23—Michael A. Hampshire. 25 through 31—Paintings by Michael A. Hampshire. 32—Hirmer Fotoarchiv, Munich. 35—General Research and Humanities Division, The New York Public Library, Astor, Lenox and Tilden Foundations. 37—Max G. Scheler from Magnum—General Research and Humanities Division, The New York Public Library, Astor, Lenox and Tilden Foundations. 40—Ullstein, Berlin. 45—Michael A. Hampshire (top). 46, 47—General Research and Humanities Division, The New York Public Library, Astor, Lenox and Tilden Foundations—Michael A. Hampshire. 48, 49—Hirmer Fotoarchiv, Munich; General Research and Humanities Division, The New York Public Library, Astor, Lenox and Tilden Foundations. 50—General Research and Humanities Division, The New York Public Library, Astor, Lenox and Tilden Foundations; Michael A. Hampshire. 51, 52—Hirmer Fotoarchiv, Munich. 55—The Walters Art Gallery. 56, 57—Staatliche Museen zu Berlin, Vorderasiatisches Museum Abt. 59—Max G. Scheler from Magnum. 60, 61—Courtesy of the Oriental Institute, University of Chicago. 63—Courtesy Dr. Franz Steinherr, Munich. 65—Roland Michaud from Rapho Guillumette. 66—Fulvio Roiter. 67—Dmitri Kessel, TIME-LIFE Picture Agency, © 1972 Time Incorporated. 68, 69—Ara Guler. 70—Mustafa Türkyilmaz. 71—Roland and Sabrina Michaud from Rapho Guillumette. 72—Photo F. L. Kenett, Copyright George Rainbird Ltd., 1963. 75—C.F.A. Schaeffer. 77—By courtesy of the Israel Department of Antiquities and Museums—The Metropolitan Museum of Art, Museum Excavations, 1910-1911, Rogers Fund, 1911. 79—Slavonic Division, The New York Public Library, Astor, Lenox and Tilden Foundations. 83—Brian Brake from Rapho Guillumette. 84 through 89—W. Wreszinski: *Atlas zur Altaegyptischen Kulturgeschichte* Vol. 2. Leipzig: Hinrichs Verlag, 1935, courtesy Oriental Division, The New York Public Library, Astor, Lenox and Tilden Foundations. 90—Josephine Powell. 93—From Ippolito Rosellini, *I Monumenti dell'Egitto e della Nubia,* Pisa, Presso N. Capurro, 1832-1844. 96, 97—Hirmer Fotoarchiv, Munich courtesy Ankara Archaeological Museum except bottom right Ankara Archaeological Museum. 98—From Riemschneider, *Die Welt der Hethiter,* Cotta-Verlag. 100—Ankara Archaeological Museum. 102—Ashmolean Museum, Oxford. 105 through 113—Drawings by Michael A. Hampshire. 114—Hirmer Fotoarchiv, Munich courtesy Ankara Archaeological Museum. 116—Professor Rudolf Naumann, Deutsches Archaeologisches Institut, Istanbul. 119—Hirmer Fotoarchiv, Munich. 120—Mustafa Türkyilmaz; Drawing by Adolph E. Brotman from Rudolf Naumann's *Architektur Kleinasiens.* 121—Scala—Drawings by Adolph E. Brotman from Rudolf Naumann's *Architektur Kleinasiens.* 122—Hirmer Fotoarchiv, Munich except bottom right drawing by Adolph E. Brotman from Rudolf Naumann's *Architektur Kleinasiens.* 126—Fulvio Roiter. 127—From *Hattusha: The Capital of the Hittites* by Kurt Bittel. Copyright © 1970 by Oxford University Press, Inc. Figure 13 on p. 56, plan of Temple I. 131 through 137—Drawings by James Alexander. 138—Hirmer Fotoarchiv, Munich. 140—Hirmer Fotoarchiv, Munich courtesy Ankara Archaeological Museum. 141—Hirmer Fotoarchiv, Munich courtesy Adana Museum. 145—Valerie Stalder. 147, 148, 149—Ozan Sagdic courtesy Ankara Archaeological Museum. 150—Roland Michaud from Rapho Guillumette courtesy Ankara Archaeological Museum; Valerie Stalder courtesy Adana Museum. 151—Courtesy of the Trustees of the British Museum. 152, 153—Ozan Sagdic courtesy Ankara Archaeological Museum.

Acknowledgments

For the help given in the preparation of this book, the editors are indebted to Ekrem Akurgal, Professor of Hittitology, and Tahsin Ozgüç, Rector, University of Ankara, Turkey; Pierre Amiet, Chief Curator, Department of Oriental Antiquities, Louvre Museum, Paris; Kurt Bittel, Professor, Heidenheim-Brenz, former Director, German Archeological Institute, Berlin; British Museum, Department of Western Asiatics; Sevim Bülüc, Curator, Middle East Technical University Museum; Halet Cambel, Professor of Archeology, Istanbul University, Turkey; Henry Fischer, Research Curator, Metropolitan Museum of Art, New York City; Rolf Hachmann, Professor of Prehistory, University of Saarbrücken, Germany; J. D. Hawkins, Lecturer in Ancient Anatolian Languages, University of London; Emmanuel Laroche, Member of the French Institute, Director, French Institute of Archeology at Istanbul; Gerhard Rudolf Meyer, Director, State Museum of Berlin; Rudolf Naumann, Director, German Archeological Institute at Istanbul; C.F.A. Schaeffer, Member of the French Institute, Honorary Professor at the College of France; Hande Surmelioglu, Deputy Director, Turkish Tourism and Information Office, New York City; Raci Temizer, Archeological Museum, Ankara, Turkey.

Bibliography

Akurgal, Ekrem, *Ancient Civilizations and Ruins of Turkey.* Translated by John Whybrow and Mollie Emre. Mobil Oil Turk A. S., 1969.

The Art of the Hittites. Translated by Constance McNab. Thames and Hudson, 1962.

Bittel, Kurt, *Guide to Bogazköy.* Archaeological Museum of Ankara.

Hattusha: The Capital of the Hittites. Oxford University Press, 1970.

Boudet, Jacques, ed., *The Ancient Art of Warfare,* Vol. I. Robert Laffont, 1966.

Breasted, James Henry, *Decennial Publications of the University of Chicago.* University of Chicago Press, 1903.

A History of Egypt from the Earliest Times to the Persian Conquest. Charles Scribner's Sons, 1912.

Budge, Sir E. A. Wallis, *By Nile and Tigris: A Narrative of Journeys in Egypt.* John Murray, 1879.

Burckhardt, John Lewis, *Travels in Syria and the Holy Land.* John Murray, 1822.

Ceram, C. W., *Narrow Pass, Black Mountain.* Translated by Richard and Clara Winston. Sidgwick and Jackson Limited, 1956.

The Secret of the Hittites. Translated by Richard and Clara Winston. Alfred A. Knopf, 1956.

ed., *The World of Archaeology: The Pioneers Tell Their Own Story.* Thames and Hudson, 1966.

Cowley, A. E., *The Hittites: The Schweich Lectures for 1918.* By H. Milford for the Oxford University Press, 1920.

Davidson, Marshall B., ed., *The Horizon Book of Lost Worlds.* American Heritage Publishing Co., 1962.

Desroches-Noblecourt, Christiane, *Tutankhamen.* New York Graphic Society, 1963.

Doblhofer, Ernst, *Voices in Stone: The Decipherment of Ancient Scripts and Writings.* Translated by Mervyn Savill. Collier Books, 1971.

Du Ry, Carel J., *Art of the Ancient Near and Middle East.* Harry N. Abrams, Inc., 1969.

Erman, Adolf, *Life in Ancient Egypt.* Translated by H. M. Tirard. Macmillan and

Co., 1894.
Frankfort, Henri, ed., *The Art and Architecture of the Ancient Orient*, from *The Pelican History of Art*. Penguin Books, 1970.
Garstang, John, *The Hittite Empire*. Richard R. Smith Inc., 1930.
Gordon, Cyrus H., *Forgotten Scripts: How They Were Deciphered and Their Impact on Contemporary Culture*. Basic Books, Inc., 1968.
Gurney, O. R., *The Hittites*. Penguin Books, 1972.
Hoffner, Harry A., Jr., *Food Production in Hittite Asia Minor*. American Oriental Society, 1973.
Kitchen, K. A., *Suppiluliuma and the Amarna Pharaohs: A Study in Relative Chronology*. Liverpool University Press, 1962.
Kramer, Samuel Noah, ed., *Mythologies of the Ancient World*. Doubleday & Company, Inc., 1961.
Lloyd, Seton, *Early Highland Peoples of Anatolia*. McGraw-Hill Book Co., 1967.
Mellink, Machteld, *Art Treasures of Turkey*. Smithsonian Institution, 1966.
Montgomery, Field-Marshal Bernard Law, *A History of Warfare*. The World Publishing Company, 1968.
Neufeld, E., *The Hittite Laws*. Luzac & Co. Ltd., 1951.
Petrie, W. M. Flinders, *Syria and Egypt from the Tell el Amarna Letters*. Methuen & Co., 1898.
Tell el Amarna. Methuen & Co., 1894.
Pritchard, James B., ed., *The Ancient Near East in Pictures Relating to the Old Testament*. Princeton University Press, 1954.
ed., *Ancient Near Eastern Texts Relating to the Old Testament*. Princeton University Press, 1969.
Roux, Georges, *Ancient Iraq*. Penguin Books, 1972.
Sayce, A. H., *The Hittites: The Story of a Forgotten Empire*. The Religious Tract Society, 1892.
Reminiscences. Macmillan and Co., 1923.
Stark, Freya and Fulvio Roiter, *Gateways and Caravans: A Portrait of Turkey*. The Macmillan Company, 1971.
Temizer, Raci, *Museum of Anatolian Civilizations*. Archaeological Museum of Ankara, 1973.
Vieyra, Maurice, *Hittite Art*. Alec Tiranti Ltd., 1955.
Westendorf, Wolfhart, *Painting, Sculpture, and Architecture of Ancient Egypt*. Harry N. Abrams, Inc., 1968.
Wiseman, D. J., ed., *Peoples of Old Testament Times*. Oxford at the Clarendon Press, 1973.
Wright, William, *The Empire of the Hittites*. James Nisbet & Co., 1884.
Yadin, Yigael, *The Art of Warfare in Biblical Lands*, Vols. 1 and 2. McGraw-Hill Book Co., 1963.

Index

Numerals in italics indicate an illustration of the subject mentioned.

Printed in U.S.A.